Martin Walsh

The Brechtian Aspect of Radical Cinema

edited by Keith M. Griffiths

bfi

1981
BFI Publishing

Published by the British Film Institute
127 Charing Cross Road
London WC2H 0EA
Copyright © British Film Institute 1981
Individual articles © original source
Cover Design: Atelier Koninck, Londyn

Printed by Tonbridge Printers Ltd
Shipbourne Road, Tonbridge, Kent
British Library Cataloguing in Publication Data
Walsh, Martin
   The Brechtian aspect of radical cinema
   1. Moving-pictures 2. Radicalism
   I. Title II. Griffiths, Keith M.
   791.43'75   PN1995.9.R

ISBN 0-85170-111-6
ISBN 0-85170-112-4 Pbk

Contents

Acknowledgments
Introduction by Keith M. Griffiths   1
The Complex Seer: Brecht and the Film   5
The Political Joke in «Happiness»   22
Political Formations in the Cinema of Jean-Marie Straub   37
«History Lesson»: Brecht and Straub/Huillet   60
«Introduction to Arnold Schoenberg's ‹Accompaniment for a
    Cinematographic Scene› »   78
«Moses and Aaron»: Straub and Huillet's Schoenberg   91
Losey, Brecht and «Galileo»   108
Godard and Me: Jean-Pierre Gorin Talks   116
Draft Outline: The Brechtian Aspect of Radical Cinema   129
Martin Walsh: Biography and Articles Published   132
References   134
Further Reading   135

Acknowledgments

I should like to thank Angela Martin and Geoffrey Nowell-Smith for their assistance and support in compiling and editing this collection of essays; Stephen Heath for his advice on the structure; Mr and Mrs Walsh for all their help and patience and for giving me access to Martin's files and papers; Gwyn Rhydderch for her encouragement; Roma Gibson, Erich Sargeant, the National Film Archive/Stills Library, the American Film Theater, Universal Edition, the Other Cinema, and Andi and Pam Engel for their assistance with the stills and photographs; Greg Curnoe for his drawing of Martin, and the Brothers Quaij (Atelier Koninck) for the design of the cover and text; the Goethe Institute for their wonderful reference library; and in particular all those magazines and journals who have kindly allowed us to reprint Martin's essays in this book.

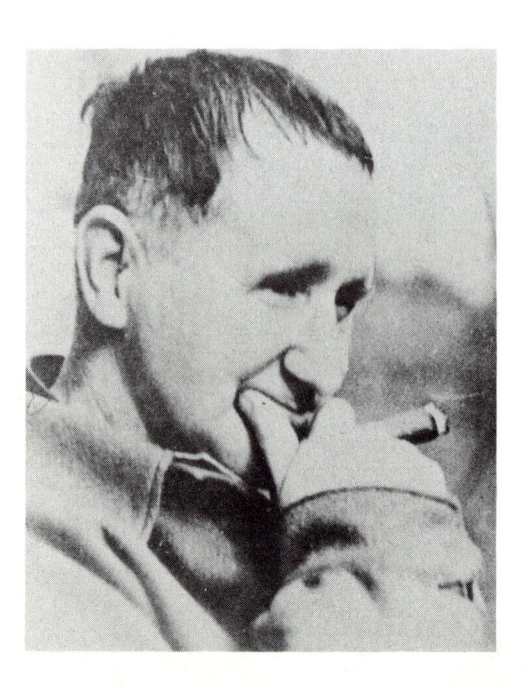

Introduction by Keith M. Griffiths

Martin Walsh died in the summer of 1977 following a tragic cycling accident near London, Ontario, Canada, where he had been living and working since 1972. During this five-year period he taught film at the University of Western Ontario and made a major contribution to the development of film studies both at the University and throughout the province. For three years he had been President of the Film Studies Association of Ontario and had recently become a founder member of the editorial board of *Ciné-tracts,* the now established Canadian journal of film and communications theory published in Montreal. Previously Martin had developed in his essays for other periodicals, particularly in the USA, a rarely found skill for making the difficult and complex area of «radical cinema» more widely accessible.

Since 1974 he had devoted considerable time to research on the influence of Brecht's thought on contemporary European film-making. This involved Brecht's relationship to the film industries of Germany and Hollywood, the connections between Soviet avant-garde theory of the 20s and early 30s and Brecht's own work in that period. To this was coupled a close study of the films of Jean-Marie Straub and Danièle Huillet. At the now «historic» Brecht Event at the Edinburgh film festival in 1975, Martin chaired an open discussion with Straub and Huillet. This meeting considerably focused his ideas, his future teaching practice and his critical writing. On his return to Canada and through the long snowbound winter of 1975–6, Martin worked on the outline of a book proposal under the title *The Brechtian Aspect of Radical Cinema.*

Unfortunately Martin was not able to begin the book before he died. He did, however, leave us a number of contributions to film journals and periodicals which were largely consistent with the train of his thought for the project. The background to it can be seen in his «Brecht and the Film», first published in *Sight and Sound* (Autumn 1974), and many of the articles and essays, in particular those for *Jump Cut,* can be seen as the basis of various chapters. In editing this collection of his writings I have, therefore, chosen only those essays which outline and expand on this thesis. The original outline was amongst his notes (see p. 128).

Martin was concerned to unravel some of the most distinctive strands of the history of a «political» cinema that could be seen as constituting a «Brechtian tradition». He considered that the elements of this tradition cut forcefully across the national boundaries and cultures so often used to encapsulate phases of cinematic practice. Interestingly the official and sometimes governmental opposition, the problems of raising money for production, and the problems of exhibition and distribution which these film-makers have all had to confront in different ways, could be seen as reiterating Brecht's own state of permanent exile. To Martin, this fact served to cement the ties between the various directors as well as to underline the continuity of their essential direction, which he summarised as forcing «society to confront itself, and thus bring art back into a significant relationship with the process of living». It was important, therefore, to clarify the conceptual unity that embraced such otherwise divergent experiences.

The intention was to trace a strand of aesthetic enquiry back over a period of some fifty years. He hoped that the study of certain film-makers who had often been perceived as renegade or eccentric could reveal instead a persistent and wiry strand of film history, a strand devoted to the rapprochement of film and society. However, Martin was very conscious that to place film-makers as diverse as Eisenstein, Vertov, Medvedkin, Godard, Makavejev and Straub within a framework entitled «Brechtian» was to lay himself open to the danger of nullifying the uniqueness of each director's work in order to imprison the films in an alien structure. But, he wrote in his notes, «the greatest quality of Brecht's thought is its refusal of doctrine, of dogma. It offers a certain number of general principles, but even these are implicity tentative and invite questioning. Process, re-evaluation, reformulation, evolution: these are the notions that matter.»

Thus the work of those directors represented in the outline offers a series of «variations» on the premiss that the artist-audience relationship need not be a hierarchical one. For the films of this «radical strand» invite the spectator, in various ways, to think about, reflect on what s/he sees, and place it against his/her own experiences. There are no answers, only questions, and the audience's capacity to engage in a process of discovery is of primary importance.

Inevitably, there are large areas of the proposed book which Martin did not have an opportunity to develop, except as notes for his lectures at the university, and he was never to complete any significant writing on Eisenstein, Godard or Makavejev. There was an early article on the latter, published in *Monogram*, but while interesting, it is not of a comparable standard to his later work. The interview with Gorin throws an intriguing perspective on the short working relationship between himself and Godard and on the making of *Tout va bien* in particular, but he had not written anything about Godard's other work. Martin was preparing essays on Chaplin and Vertov, but the sketches in his files were not extensive enough to edit or quote from. However, the essays that were completed – particularly those on Straub/Huillet and, in my view, specifically the study of *Moses and Aaron* — reveal a remarkable talent at work. Inevitably perhaps, it is ironic that this brilliant and stunningly beautiful film is unlikely ever to be shown again in Britain because of legal and copyright complications.

Having known Martin as a close friend for most of his life, I think that there are aspects of his education and experience which throw light on the attributes of his critical work. Foremost was his ability to present the film-making process, in a critical manner but at the same time without further mystifying it. This ability undoubtedly owed much to his studies at the Film Department of the Slade School of Fine Art under Thorold Dickinson, as well as to his own enthusiasm for learning and understanding the skills of film-making and photography. He assisted Lutz Becker on his two notable Arts Council documentaries (*Kinetics* and *Art and Revolution*), and film-makers like Stan Brakhage, Straub and Huillet, and Gorin were not only visitors to his unique timber-clad house, but victims of his curiosity about film stock, lenses, laboratories and editing. The accumulation of this knowledge of and interest in the techniques of film-making is rare in a critic (with the possible exceptions of Noël Burch, Laura Mulvey and Peter Wollen, whose work Martin greatly admired). It gave his writing a special edge, which is particularly clear in his essays on Medvedkin's *Happiness* and Straub/Huillet's *Moses and Aaron* and *History Lessons*.

The essays also manage significantly to situate the «cultural» context of the films' production. He shows that many of those films whose «novelty» was seen as disturbing or contentious actually fitted into a more «international» pattern of modernist work in which cinematic ideas can often be related both to similar concerns in other fields of art-work and to various social tensions. These relationships are still frequently forgotten and in his writing Martin was always anxious to expand the framework within which the cinema, and in particular the avant-garde, is examined. He himself was an eclectic and avid collector of modernist bric-à-brac. His house was jammed with graphics, poster art, photographs, paintings, a vast collection of reggae, jazz and electronic music and the work of Ian Hamilton Finlay who finds himself woven into the essay on *History Lessons*. This enthusiasm and commitment to modernism is nicely represented in Canadian artist Greg Curnoe's portrait of Martin drawn shortly after he died.

His house was also filled with Africana — a unique collection of weaving, pottery, jewellery, drums, sculpture, mostly obtained during two trips to Africa, which had had a profound effect on him. The first was a long and arduous expedition across the Sahara to the Cameroons. During this expedition he made two documentary films: one for the BBC series *Chronicle* on the Hoggar Plateau in the Sahara, the other an anthropological film on the Gbaya tribe. The second trip was a photographic assignment to West Africa (Nigeria, Togo, Dahomey, Ghana) and resulted in a highly personal essay

(*Man Likes His Own Life*), which nevertheless attempted to reveal some of the specific contradictions inherent in the benefits and attendant horrors of Western economic aid and advice. The «essay» toured small galleries in Britain and prompted a stormy debate with African students at Western Ontario about the representation of such problems by visiting white «photo-journalists». This confrontation was crucial to his thinking about representation and the cinema. Indeed, the impact of Africa was altogether shattering, and Martin often indicated that were he to «start all over» he would want to study anthropology.

These varied aspects of Martin's life and interests, and his isolation in Canada from the theoretical mayhem affecting British film culture at the time, gave him a rather unique opportunity to develop his writing in a way that might have been impossible in London, England. The discipline of addressing a large readership made him very conscious of his presentation both in terms of style and content. The editors of *Jump Cut*, in particular, always engage their contributors in a critical discussion about their work as part of a political process which, while often stormy, is clearly constructive and helpful to both sides. The process certainly sharpened Martin's writing and contributed to its colour and individuality. To those who knew Martin Walsh, he will probably always be remembered as a wonderfully engaging and friendly English «hippie freak». More permanently, he left us after only a short academic life some remarkably lucid essays whose accessibility offers genuine insights into an area of the cinema frequently shrouded in impenetrable linguistic mysticism.

The essays that appear in this book are largely as they were originally published. Occasionally, short passages cut for reasons of space have been reinserted when they seemed helpful to the clarification of certain points. Where cuts have been made, they are primarily to try to avoid repetition and are indicated.

The Complex Seer: Brecht and the Film

Any comprehensive attempt to assess the nature of Brecht's relationship to the cinema would have to explore four quite distinct areas of investigation. The first of these (briefly) concerns Brecht's use of film fragments within the context of his theatrical presentations. The second would concentrate on Brecht's entanglement with the film industry itself in Germany (in the early 1930s) as well as in America (during the 1940s). The third would examine the possible influence of film artists such as Eisenstein and Chaplin on the initial formulation of Brecht's theories of epic theatre. The fourth – and ultimately the most crucial in terms of its contribution to aesthetic thinking in the twentieth century – is concerned less with Brecht's actual contacts with film as a material of expression, than with the impact of his theoretical writings on a generation of European directors whose collective body of work since 1960 constitutes an achievement as momentous, historically and aesthetically, as that of the Cubist painters fifty years before. The films of Jean-Luc Godard, of Jean-Marie Straub, of Dusan Makavejev, of Ruy Guerra, of Nagisa Oshima and others, all, though in various and sometimes divergent ways, bear the clear imprint of Brechtian principles. The elaboration of this latter assertion must await another occasion; here I take my task to be to sketch an outline of Brecht's personal contacts with the film medium, and then to locate his thought within a larger context of European thinking in order to explain his exemplary significance for a particular strand of film-making.

The best known (and ultimately the least important) of Brecht's contacts with the cinema revolves round his use of film as an integral element of the staging of his plays. Following the example of Piscator, Brecht found not only that «the film was a new gigantic actor that helped to narrate events . . . by means of which simultaneous events in different places could be seen together», but that «the use of the film projection» helped «bring the social complex of the events taking place to the forefront». (Brecht, 1964a, pp.78–9) Thus at the end of *Mother Courage,* Mother marches in front of a screen on which footage is projected from *October* and *The End of St. Petersburg,* as well as documentary images of Lenin, Stalin and Mao.

What we must note here is not simply the bringing of «the social complex» into the forefront, but also the calculated disjunction of conventional theatrical illusion. A tension is set up between the presence of an actor and the presence of an autonomous series of images on a screen; the relationship between the two is not internally motivated; their co-presence is not explicable in terms of dramatic necessity; rather, it is a deliberately interruptive mechanism, a mechanism that *demands* that the audience sit up and reflect on its significance. This usage is an integral part of Brecht's thrust towards «objectification», his desire to establish ruptures and tensions that make explicit his rejection of the common notion of theatre as a passive experience. In this sense, Brecht's use of film parallels his use of songs to break the continuity of the action, of gestic acting, and of the results of the «electrification» of theatrical mechanics: projected titles, moving platforms on the stage, and so on. Brecht's interest in film is simply as an extension of the expressive possibilities of the theatre — there is little apparent interest in the exploration of cinematic potential *per se* in his theatrical practice.

If Brecht's use of film in his own creative endeavours earns no more than a footnote in film history, we can claim little more significance for his forays into the world of feature film-making, since each project (from Brecht's point of view) degenerated into aesthetic disaster. But these encounters are worth examination, since the problems Brecht confronted illuminate the schism between his aesthetic and that of the narrative film tradition as it mainly evolved in Europe and America.

The first of Brecht's ventures into cinema (with the exception of some screenplays he reputedly wrote in the 20s, but which have since disappeared) occured in 1930, when it was proposed that one of his plays should be adapted for the screen. This was *The Threepenny Opera*, and G. W. Pabst was slated to direct. Brecht's play, to use his own words, «is concerned with bourgeois conceptions, not only as *content* by representing them, but also through the manner in which it does so». (Brecht, 1964a, p.43; emphasis by M. W.) That is to say, it is not enough to discuss radical or revolutionary ideas — they must be discussed in a new format. This realisation was made explicit by Walter Benjamin, the German critic and close friend of Brecht, when he lectured in Paris in 1934. Benjamin said that:

> *Transmitting an apparatus of production without — as much as possible — transforming it, is a highly debatable procedure even when the content of the apparatus which is transmitted seems to be revolutionary. In point of fact we are faced with a situation — for which the last decade in Germany furnishes complete proof — in which the bourgeois apparatus of production and publication can assimilate an astonishing number of revolutionary themes, and can even propagate them without seriously placing its own existence or the existence of the class that possesses them into question.* (Benjamin, 1970, p.90)

The truth of this becomes immediately apparent if we shift our focus momentarily to the welter of «political» films with which the American film industry has saturated the down-town cinemas over the past five years; by the very nature of their presentation as commercial entertainment narratives within the context of plush theatres, any potential «radicalising» impulse is efficiently anaesthetised. Benjamin's «apparatus of production» embraces not only the conditions of transmission of the work, however, but also its formal, technical aspect. The traditional *forms* of expression must also be transformed, and here we may note a particular closeness between the approaches of Benjamin and Brecht.

Certainly it was Brecht's *formal* innovations in The Threepenny Opera that marked the play as a radical work. Again let me quote Brecht's own notes on the play:

> *So far as the communication of the subject-matter is concerned, the spectator must not be misled along the path of empathy . . . the actor address himself directly to the spectator . . . When he sings, the actor accomplishes a change in function. Nothing is more detestable than when an actor gives the impression of not having noticed that he has left the gound of plain speech and is already singing. The three levels – plain speech, heightened speech and singing must always remain separate from one another . . . Complex seeing must be practised.* (Brecht, 1964b, pp.99/103/106)

When Pabst's film of The Threepenny Opera was released in 1931, it was apparent that it was precisely these formal aspects that had been eliminated in the transposition of Brecht's script to the screen. Although several actors from the original stage production appeared in the film, although the songs were sung by actors trained in Brecht's singing techniques, and although the costume style was faithful to Brecht's production, Pabst's mode of articulation undercut Brecht's epic, objectifying thrust. Pabst's interest in the romantic aspects of the story, his attempt to create a «hovering phantom world» through the luscious pans and travelling shots of his mobile camera, his emphasis on chiaroscuro lighting – all these aspects coalesce to produce a work which, while satisfying in its own way,* utterly lacks Brecht's abrasive satiric edge. Whereas Brecht's placards and austere mathematical sets gave a sense of immediacy, of provocation, of shock, Pabst's use of Andreiev's set designs resulted in something closer to baroque ornamentalism, enabling Lotte Eisner to effuse in The Haunted Screen:

> *Swirls of dust and smoke wreathe the dwellings of the beggar king, and cling to the bare walls, where wretches' rags are like ornamental blobs of paint, and hover in the*

---

*It is perhaps worth observing that Pabst's «alterations» to Brecht's script are perfectly consonant with the critical assumptions of the «auteur» theory. In its own terms, and within the total context of Pabst's work, The Threepenny Opera stands as a major piece of work, However, elucidation of Pabst's achievement is not my purpose here, and I shall let my bias in Brecht's favour stand.

«The Threepenny Opera»

nuptial shed on the docks, softening the splendour of the tables brimming with fruit and silverware amid the reflections of the gentle candlelight. (Eisner, 1969, p. 317)

To clinch the subversion of Brecht's intentions, Kurt Weill's songs are reduced to embellishments in the film, instead of constituting its pivotal points. Pabst does this very simply: although the songs are sung in a manner not wholly incompatible with Brecht's methods, their narrative centrality is slashed by the way in which Pabst minimises their *visual* presence on the screen. In the opening of the film, for instance, the «Mack the Knife» song merely functions as a backdrop to the nascent love affair between Mack and Polly, as Pabst concentrates on Mack lasciviously eyeing Polly.

Not surprisingly, Brecht sued the production company for what he saw as a negation of the ideological and stylistic substance of his work, and the case of «Brecht v. Nero Films» became a *cause célèbre* in Berlin. Brecht lost his case — the details of which need not concern us here. What did come out of the trial, however, was Brecht's only sustained piece of writing on the cinema; and, significantly, he rejects consideration of film aesthetic and theory, preferring instead to examine the relationships between law, art and the economic substructure.

The court's verdict established that when Brecht sold the rights of *The Threepenny Opera* to Nero films, he thereby forfeited his right to control the content of his work, on the grounds that were this *not* the case, success of the economic enterprise represented by the film industry would be jeopardised. Brecht's response was a Marxist critique of the capitalist foundations of the cinema, an exposure of its principles of exploitation. He pointed out what, thirty years later, became a primary concern of both the American Independent Cinema and the French New Wave: that the capitalist foundations of cinematic practice efficiently removed a means of expression from the grasp of a whole stratum of creative artists. Access to the medium is controlled by capitalist expediency, which thus becomes a form of political censorship (through suppression), at the very time when the persuasive potentials of audio-visual media were being fully recognised — Hitler commissioned Leni Riefenstahl's *Triumph of the Will* just four years later (having first, ironically, banned Pabst's *The Threepenny Opera* when he came to power in 1933).

What Brecht demanded was that both the courts and the critics should reconsider the social function of film:

> *As long as the social function is not criticised, then all film criticism is symptomatic criticism and itself has a symptomatic character. It exhausts itself on questions of taste and remains completely imprisoned in class prejudice. It never recognises that taste is merchandise and the weapon of a particular class, but rather it sets taste up as an absolute (which everyone has access to, which everyone can buy, even if, in fact, everyone cannot pay).* (Brecht, 1972, p.37)

It is here, more clearly than almost anywhere else in his writing, that

Brecht's communist commitment is expressed; and shortly afterwards, in late 1931, Brecht began work on the script of *Kuhle Wampe,* known in the West as *Whither Germany?*. The film was partly financed by a Russian company, and it gained instant notoriety as the only communist film to be made in Germany during the 30s. It was predictably banned (though a cut version was subsequently exhibited), and is difficult to see today.* But its subtitle, *To whom does the world belong?*, clearly hints at its subject matter, and accounts suggest that Brecht succeeded in transmitting his ideological beliefs to the screen. He and the director Slatan Dudow worked closely and apparently harmoniously together, and the film managed to make its general social statement: the censor complained that one of its central events, the suicide of a young worker, was presented provocatively as typical of the destiny of a whole class, rather than simply as the tragic destiny of a particular individual! Stylistically, however, the film appears to be fairly conventional, having none of the innovatory spirit that characterised the formal aspects of Brecht's stage work.

Brecht had no further involvement with film-making until he arrived in Los Angeles in 1941; shortly thereafter he began work with his compatriot in exile, Fritz Lang, on *Hangmen Also Die.* And again the experience was an unhappy one. Although it was not to be expected that Lang's dourly fatalistic vision (*M,* or *You Only Live Once,* for example) could be reconciled with Brecht's progressive experimentalism, the problem was further compounded by the fact that, since Brecht spoke little English, another writer, John Wexley, had to be called in to assist. Inevitably conflicts arose, and the accounts vary. Some claim Wexley demanded sole screen credit, and was granted it by the Screen Writers Guild; others claim that Brecht refused to have his name credited, allowing only «from an idea by Brecht», because of what he considered a substantial distortion of his intention.

From this point on, it is clear that Brecht regarded his work in the cinema as simply a means to earn his living. Hollywood was always eager to secure «name» writers, and Brecht churned out scripts, which were so chewed over in the studio factories that his ideas were invariably modified beyond recognition. A good example is *Arch of Triumph,* made in 1947 by Lewis Milestone, and adapted from a novel by E. M. Remarque. Remarque was a German writer who, like Pabst, belonged to the «New Objectivity» school which Walter Benjamin scathingly characterised by saying that «It has even succeeded in making misery itself an object of pleasure, by treating it stylishly and with technical perfection.» (Benjamin op. cit., p.90) It is hardly surprising that a Hollywood studio should feel attracted to such material, but it is ironic that Brecht should have found himself caught in the process of transposition. He was always given German materials to work with, and the studio bosses

---

*Now available on 16mm from Artificial Eye, 211 Camden High Street, London NW1.

evidently felt that national identity was sufficient foundation for success. But this clearly was not the case, ideological, philosophical and aesthetic compatibility being necessary elements that Brecht never found in his dealings with the cinema. As he wrote sadly in a poem entitled «Hollywood» (Brecht, 1976, p.382):

Every day to earn my daily bread
I go to the nearest market where lies are bought
Hopefully
I take up my place among the sellers.

Economic necessities ironically, even tragically, forced him to enter the ranks of those whom he had so bitterly attacked in *The Threepenny Opera* court case. Even this, however, did not make him «safe» politically; late in 1947 he was (like Chaplin and like Joseph Losey, who directed the first American production of *Galileo*) harassed by the House Un-American Activities Committee. Testifying before the Committee before he returned to Europe in November, 1947, Brecht said, «I am unaware of any influence, political or artistic, that I could have exercised on the film industry.» (Brecht, 1973, p.5) And indeed no such influence was apparent until after his death in 1956 — and then it was not in America that it was to be found.*

After fleeing political persecution for the third time in his life (first Germany, then Finland, and finally America), it is hardly surprising that Brecht's revolutionary ardour was somewhat dampened in his later years. (This is evident if one compares his writing of the late 20s with that of the late 40s and early 50s). Indeed the image of the later Brecht is perhaps commensurate with the figure of Galileo at the end of that play: not having betrayed his past, but withdrawn from public combat. Thus it is not surprising that it is to the earlier writings that we find the radical European film directors of the 1960s turning their attention. (Godard's *Tout va bien* for instance, is explicitly indebted to Brecht's «Notes to the opera *Aufstieg und Fall der Stadt Mahagonny*».) And it is unquestionably these earlier writings that provide the link I wish to make between Brecht and a cinematic tradition that runs from Eisenstein to Godard.

The aesthetic position which Eisenstein, Brecht and Godard hold in common is a hostility to illusionism; illusionism being a mode of artistic experience that has as its most central characteristics: a desire to (psychologically) penetrate individual experience; its primary appeal is to the emotions rather than the intellect, desiring the audience's empathetic involvement with the events presented before them, in the passive manner suggested by

---

*A recent film, *A Good Example* (1980, 30 mins.), dramatically reconstructs Brecht's testimony to the HUAC. It is available from The Other Cinema, 79 Wardour Street, London W1.

Coleridge's «willing suspension of disbelief»; it has a closed form which implies a certain artistic autonomy, a self-validation; it prefers to regard the medium of expression as somehow transparent, neutral, having no «point of view» of its own; language wants to be overlooked, effaced. Brecht's theatrical practice obviously inverts *all* of these priorities, and his theoretical writings constantly stress the contemporary necessity of a rethinking of dramatic praxis. His theatre may thus be seen as a reaction against a tradition that had lasted several hundred years; a reaction against the perspectival tradition of the post-Renaissance world; which posited the eye (and man behind it) as the centre of the world, and art as a window (therefore transparent) on that world.

The «language» of art was increasingly regarded as merely an instrument through which a representation of the world was achieved – a representation which remained unaffected by the instrument itself. The history of twentieth-century art, however, provides copious examples of the rejection of this position: in painting, Cubism continued the path inaugurated by the Impressionists, in the exploration of painting as its own system, an exploration which continues through to the American Abstract Expressionists; at the root of this experimentation is the exclusion of (in Stephen Bann's words) «the traditional correspondence between the notional position of the spectator and the three-dimensional ordering of the illusory space of the work». (Bann, 1972, p. 5) In literature, Joyce's tussles with language in *Finnegans Wake,* and the more recent experiments of the «Nouveau Roman» group of Robbe-Grillet, Simon, Duras and Butor indicate a similar uneasiness with the tradition of the nineteenth-century novel; in theatre, we find Meyerhold and Brecht occupying a similarly radical position *vis-à-vis* their predecessors; and in the cinema, too, we may locate a stream of dissent against the narrative tradition. But in the cinema, this stream is comparatively small, despite its historical significance. For the camera, both still and moving, has consistently been mobilised in support of an «ideology of the visible»: as Jean-Louis Comolli* has pointed out, the image produced by the camera could not fail to confirm and reinforce «the visual code defined by Renaissance humanism» which placed the human eye at the centre of the system of representation.

A code of realism thus grew up very rapidly. A Dublin poster for the first screenings of the Lumière films in 1896 proclaims that their images are «so realistic that for the moment one is almost apt to forget that the representation is artificial». During the next sixty years, the primary aim of the film industry (apart from making money – or in order to make money) was increased realism (visual and psychological), as the successive developments of film technology indicate: panchromatic film stock replaced orthochromatic because it was sensitive to a wider range of colours through the spectrum – it was more

---

*See Comolli's series of essays under the heading «Technique and Ideology» in *Cahiers du Cinéma,* No. 229, 1971 and subsequent issues.

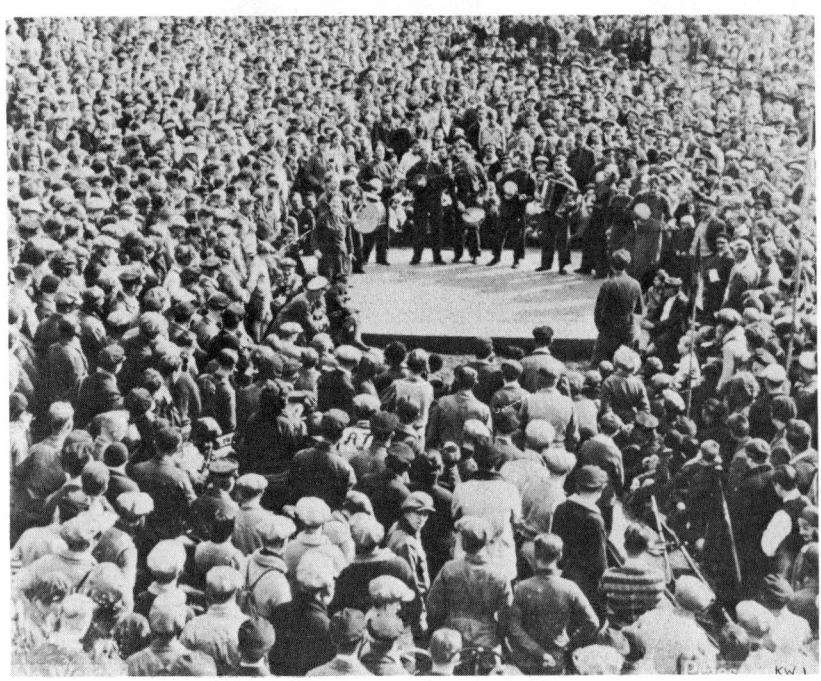

«Kuhle Wampe»

«realistic»; colour was hailed as an advance in realism, as were sound and wide screen. André Bazin's aesthetic doctrine rested on the virtues of deep focus cinematography, since deep focus, for him, respected the «integrity» of visual space; and the critical orthodoxy represented by Bazin valued «realistic» directors such as Murnau and Welles over the montage school inaugurated by the Soviet directors of the 20s.*

The concomitant of this valuation of «realistic» cinema is the affirmation of illusionist aesthetics. Films such as Murnau's *Sunrise* (hailed by critics of the time as greatest film ever made) evince precisely the qualities that Brecht and Eisenstein (and, much later, Godard) reacted against: psychological penetration of character; an organic, closed structure; conservative ethic of hero and heroine reunited through benign fate, or optimism in the final triumph of «human nature»; a technique of stylistic self-effacement that refuses to interrupt the identificatory propulsion towards catharsis — the use of *trompe l'oeil* backdrops, carefully painted to reassert perspectival laws, and hence reality, emphasises the desire to *hide* technique. Against this, we may contrast Brecht's desire to «show the machinery, the ropes, and the flies», as does «a sporting arena during a boxing match», and to make visible the sources of light for that set. (Brecht, 1964a, p.233)** At the root of Brecht's antipathy toward illusionism is his oft-stated opinion that «Feelings are private and limited. Against that the reason is fairly comprehensive and to be relied on.» (ibid., p.15) From this base, Brecht's formulation of the principles of epic theatre evolved as the simple antithesis of illusionist precepts: the generic focus of epic replaces the individualist focus of most dramatic and lyric art; intellectual activity replaces emotional involvement; the audience becomes the co-creator of the work, rather than its receptacle.

Only in Russia, in the years immediately after the Soviet Revolution, do we find an approach to cinema that matches Brecht's particular rejection of illusionism. And in fact I think it is reasonable to suggest that Brecht's aesthetic theories were themselves partially formulated as a response to his encounters with the Soviet avant-garde of Meyerhold, Tretyakov, Eisenstein, Vertov, Mayakovsky and others. For in Russia after the Revolution, film was welcomed as a new art outside the perspectival/illusionist tradition; its technological, mechanical base was embraced by the constructivist artists, and film's ability artificially to create a world through montage, rather than

---

*The fact that this orthodoxy is increasingly falling into disrepute today (i.e. it is difficult now to perceive Murnau and Welles as primarily «realistic» directors) does not invalidate the point; through the 40s and 50s what was valued in film was *expressed* in terms of «realism».
**It is interesting to note in parenthesis that one of Eisenstein's first stage productions (*The Mexican,* inspired by Jack London) included a boxing match. Instead of having the fight offstage, in the conventional manner, Eisenstein had his actors learn how to box, and incorporated the boxing match into the text of the performance; the stage became a sporting arena.

through a conventional re-creation of reality, was rapidly grasped. In 1923, for instance, Dziga Vertov published a manifesto in *Lef* bewailing the lack of «a single picture . . . directed . . . towards the emancipation of the film camera, which remains wretchedly enslaved, subordinated to the imperfect, undiscerning human eye». (Vertov, 1971, p. 52) Aware of the dominant presence of a naturalistic aesthetic, Vertov demanded the «dislocation and concentration of visual phenonema» (analogous, obviously, to Brecht's alienation effect), and proclaimed: «From today we are liberating the camera, and making it work in the opposite direction, *furthest away from copying*». (ibid,, p.53)

Vertov was not alone in his radical conception of the cinema's potential. In 1924 Eisenstein made *Strike,* a film which not only demonstrates the seminal influence of Meyerhold and Tretyakov's dramatic theories, their emphasis on the «how» of artistic expression, but marks the beginnings of a strain of cinema in which naturalism and psychological observation play no part. Brecht's formulation of «epic» theatre evolved during the late 1920s, and by that time the concept was firmly entrenched in the theatrical and cinematic praxis of a whole constellation of Soviet artists.

The key figure was Meyerhold, whose work consistently prefigures Brecht's by some years. In 1920 he bewailed the fact that «In the intimate theatres the removal of footlights has still not led to the elimination of bourgeois illusion, because in place of footlights they have bored a keyhole to satisfy the curiosity of prying spectators» (Meyerhold, 1969, p. 172); in 1923, his production of Faiko's *Lake Lyul* used advertisement hoardings, lifts and stairs as its sets, besides screens for projected titles. Meyerhold used area lighting to switch the action constantly from one level to another, and handled his scenes in an episodic manner close to the principles of montage that Eisenstein was in the process of evolving. By 1927, the influence of these artists had been sufficient to prompt an editorial in *Novy Lef* that proclaimed: «We consider that with increased precision of work in art, the epic will gain ground at the expense of the lyric.» (*Novy Lef,* 1971, p.68)

It was with *October*, on which he began work in 1926, that Eisenstein most clearly demonstrated the potential of cinematic epic.[*] One example of this epic mode in operation: the opening of the bridge. The sequence comes just after demonstrating crowds have been fired upon by the Czarist government's troops; the government orders the bridge to be opened, to cut off the demonstrators' escape. The lessons of the Cubist painters were well appreciated in Russia. Malevich, the Suprematist painter who designed sets for Meyerhold, said that he «treated space not as illusionary, but as cubist», and Meyerhold himself pronounced «We shall employ more and more Cubists and

---

[*] See Annette Michelson, «Camera Lucida/Camera Obscura» in *Artforum,* January 1973, and the essays by Noël Carroll and Rosalind Krauss in this issue, all of which explore this assertion more thoroughly.

Suprematists, and do away with the barrier of the footlights.» (op. cit., p. 174) Thus Eisenstein shoots the opening of the bridge from a wide range of angles, and many of the shots are repeated. Time is stretched out, extended, but not so as to create *tension* (as it would, for example, in Griffith). The effect is *analytic,* rather than empathetic; the multiplicity of viewpoints precludes simple audience identifications; the repetition of shots, and the use of slow motion, deliberately undercuts any tendency towards a purely naturalistic viewing of the event. The repetition establishes an air of critical investigation rather than voyeurism — an investigation of the authority that exercises its power in this inhuman manner. The temporal distension of the scene — like the Odessa Steps massacre in *Battleship Potemkin* — takes it out of time, to the extent that it assumes a kind of exemplary import: the significance of the scene is not limited to its particular locus in *this* sequence of events, but is a paradigmatic metaphor of the evils that the Revolution finally overcomes.

Other scenes, such as Kerensky's ascension to power, or the earlier interface of trench scenes with gun machinery being lowered by cranes (to «illustrate» the oppression of the soldiers by their commanders), or the «God and Country» sequence (which brilliantly *proves* in visual terms that God does not exist) are instances of Eisenstein's articulation of an epic form at its most ascetic, operating through a dialectical mode of visual argumentation. These sequences are shorn of emotional enticement — unlike the opening of the bridge, where Eisenstein's use of the dead girl's flowing hair and the dangling horse is quite calculated to tug at our heartstrings, at the same time that it trenchantly analyses the situation in more abstractly intellectual terms. This dual focus is not however incompatible with Brecht's own position. «A considerable sacrifice of the spectator's empathy does not mean sacrificing all right to influence him», Brecht wrote in 1936, continuing to note that emotional effects «are deliberate, and have to be controlled.» (Brecht, 1964a, pp. 100–1) In sum, then, we may find in *October* an extraordinary parallel to Brecht's own theories of epic theatre.

Whether Brecht's ideas were formed or confirmed through his contact with Eisenstein and his films (they had met when Eisenstein visited Berlin in 1929, and Brecht made specific reference to *Battleship Potemkin* in 1930, in the article written after the *Threepenny Opera* lawsuit), it is difficult to say. In the light of the German work of Heartfield, Grosz, Piscator and other Dadaists who ultimately rallied toward a revolutionary cause, I would suspect that Brecht's encounter with Eisenstein was principally the discovery of a kindred spirit, which underlined the co-incidence of parallel endeavours. But the cinema certainly had *some* formative influence on Brecht, who early on adapted to his own plays silent cinema's interspersion of visual sequences with printed titles.

More specifically, Brecht ardently admired Chaplin's films, as several early essays testify (and he later met Chaplin in Hollywood). Nor was Brecht alone in this; both Eisenstein and Meyerhold wrote on Chaplin's art, and in 1936 Meyerhold noted «an astonishing resemblance» (op. cit., p.311) between the work of Chaplin and Eisenstein. Although Brecht appreciated the elements of social criticism in Chaplin's films, the greater impact was a formal, methodological one: the episodic nature of Chaplin's narratives, and his selection of what Meyerhold praised as his «monumental subjects». Writing on *The Gold Rush*, Brecht commended story and theme on the ground that the average theatre would at once reject anything so simple, crude and linear. This was one aspect of Chaplin's influence; the other was his gestic acting style. Writing in 1931, Brecht said:

As against the dramatic actor, who has his character established from the first and simply exposes it to the inclemencies of the world and the tragedy, the epic actor lets his character grow before the spectator's eyes out of the way in which he behaves . . . The actor Chaplin . . . would in many ways come closer to the epic than to the dramatic theatre's requirements. (Brecht, 1964a, p.56)

In more general terms, Brecht's fondness for a low life milieu, and his emphasis on the primary role of laughter on the epic stage, may testify to Chaplin's example, and it has been observed that one of the sources for *Puntila* was *City Lights*.

Historically, however, it is the Russian avant-garde of the 20s that provides the seminal ideological and aesthetic connection with Brecht's work. Note I say «the avant-garde», rather than simply «Russian art»; the climate of artistic expression in the new Soviet society never settled into anything remotely resembling concord. This avant-garde grew out of the Futurist movement, and was in conscious opposition to the predominant tendency of support for a socially conscious realism based on the achievement of the nineteenth-century novel. In 1917, the Bolsheviks were decidedly prejudiced against the Futurists, but the vigour of the avant-garde's engagement in social concerns after the October Revolution placated that hostility. It was only a temporary placation, however, as Meyerhold's constant struggle against official suppression of his work suggested.

Thus to propose Brecht's theoretical writing in the 20s as a model of Marxist aesthetics, or his stage work as montagist, would be to encourage critical confusion. Montage, as it is commonly understood (or misunderstood) is capable of embracing equally Eisenstein, Ford, Pudovkin, Milestone. Although Walter Benjamin notes that Brecht's theoretical principles mark a return to those of «montage», he fails to make explicit the fact that (like many cinematic techniques), montage may be used in both «illusionary» and «alienatory» ways – either Ford's «invisible editing» or Eisenstein's analytic editing. The decisive difference between Eisenstein and his colleague Pudovkin means that the specification «Russian montage» serves only to conjure up a false image of harmony. Similarly, the designation «Marxist aesthetics» masks more issues than it clarifies. For there was (and is) no Marxist aesthetics: Marx never formulated one, and what passes for such covers the spectrum of socialist thinking. And even at its highest echelon we must note a decisive split, a split which has reverberated through the last fifty years, whenever the problematic relationship between art and politics has been mooted. This split may be codified by these oppositions: Meyerhold v. Stanislavsky; Eisenstein v. Pudovkin; Brecht v. Lukács; Godard v. Truffaut; Makavejev v. Widerberg.

The essential contours of this split may be sketched out through a comparison of the work of Brecht and Lukács, who remain the most influential and accessible exponents of a criticism oriented towards a Marxist commitment.* The cornerstone of Lukács' thought is the concept of «wholeness». Like Brecht, he perceives contemporary society (specifically capitalist society) as alienated, fragmented, discordant; like Brecht, he sees the function of art as being to raise (proletarian) consciousness to a point where it may actively intervene in the process of social determination, and thereby attack at the roots of that social alienation. But Lukács believes that the chaos and fragmentation of «reality» has to be overcome, transcended, in the work of art, which should present a vision of «wholeness» and «unity». The socialist writer, Lukács maintained, could look forward to a time when alienation will have been conquered, eliminated, and this awareness should be mediated through the writer's presentation of man. Lukács' only concern with the *method* of articulation, artistic technique, was that it should reinforce the «wholeness» that was the abstract *content* of the work. The function of «form» is simply to unify the elements, or fragments, of reality that the work contains, to unify them into a totality.

Lukács thus tends to see the work of art as an entity, something complete in itself. Brecht, on the other hand, rejects this concept of «closure», and with it the idea that the work of art should concern itself with «wholeness». Brecht's thrust is towards an open-ended theatrical form which makes contradiction and alienation explicit. He sees the «closure» of the work of art as itself potentially alienating, in that it perpetuates the distinction between author and audience, producer and consumer (cf. *The Threepenny Opera* lawsuit). By developing open-ended forms, and attacking the illusionist tradition, Brecht actively worked towards creative participation by the audience: they ceased to be spectators «consuming» art (as they still are in Lukács' aesthetic), and became an integral and necessary part of the production of the work. Thus matters of «form» and «technique» assume much greater importance for Brecht than for Lukács; implicit in Brecht's theory and practice is the notion

---

*For a fuller exploration of this issue (to which I am also indebted here), see *Working Papers in Cultural Studies* No. 4 (Spring 1973), the University of Birmingham.

«Hangmen also Die»

that a work of art could only be politically revolutionary if it was technically revolutionary also.

These two responses — what one might term the «avant-garde» and «conservative» variants of leftist criticism — to the recognition of «alienation» in its various manifestations (social, economic, psychological) seem to me to form the main prongs of politically committed art. And, historically, there is little doubt as to which has met with greater acceptance: the years between 1926 and 1940 in Russia proved to be years of persecution for the most excitingly radical artists of the new society. Eisenstein's great work, *October,* was contemptuously dismissed by «official» critics, who accused him of «massive subjectivism» and «quixotic digressions». Gradually the constructivist principles — the desire to create a functional art — were warped and simplified by government heads, to the point where «functional art» became synonymous with «realism»: only images of «real people» (the actual proletariat) doing «real-life things» can be functional. The kind of abstract intellectual argumentation through visual images that Eisenstein became preoccupied with, was perceived as idiosyncratic and individualist; hence unacceptable.

The reaction against Eisenstein in the late 20s hardened into suppression in the 30s; he was virtually barred from making films and at one point was forced publicly to denounce his work. Mayakovsky took refuge in suicide in 1930; Tretyakov was arrested in 1937, and killed shortly thereafter in one of Stalin's purges; Meyerhold's fate was to be the same. Lecturing in 1936, he bewailed the fact that «the celebrated formulae which were once flaunted by Eisenstein are rooted in profound principles but, as far as I can see, forgotten» (op. cit., p. 322). For «forgotten» read «suppressed»: a year later an article in the newspaper *Izvestiya* read: «Meyerhold completely refused to admit that he had encouraged sycophancy and suppressed criticism, and that his false political and artistic policies had led his theatre to total disaster.» (ibid., p.252).

His theatre was closed for the last time a few months later, and Meyerhold himself arrested; he is believed to have been shot in a Moscow prison in February 1940. From that time until the late 1950s, every trace of his name was eradicated from official histories of Soviet theatre, and his writings secreted in vaults. In short, a whole tradition of artistic investigation was effectively crushed by Stalin in the 30s (only Vertov lived through to the fifties, and he lost his freedom to work in 1937). And it is at this point that we can finally assess the crucial significance of Brecht's writings: it is through him that the line of thought first developed by certain Russian artists was continued, kept alive, until its recent, radical reformulation in the work of the European cinematic avant-garde.

Obviously the influence of Eisenstein has *always* been a seminal one for film-makers conscious of cinematic traditions; but it is doubtful whether this influence has always been for the right reasons. One indication is the orthodox preference for *Battleship Potemkin* over *October*. Not only is the former film more assimilable into critical assessments that value «organic unity» over «open-endedness», but its visual authenticity led to its valuation as one inspiration of Grierson's documentary school — the English-speaking world's version of the «new objectivity» that almost made «misery itself an object of pleasure». The inaccessibility of the theoretical texts of *Lef* and *Novy Lef* that could act as a corrective to this estimation of Eisenstein's work, and the systematic obliteration of references to Meyerhold and others, has made films like *October* seem like isolated warts on an otherwise unblemished and undistinguished proletarian cinemascape.

Until very recently, it was only through Brecht's writing that the trenchant critical edge of this particular brand of aesthetic enquiry could be perceived with conceptual clarity. This is not, of course, to suggest that Brecht's principal achievement is as a transmitter (or populariser) of certain ideas generated by the Russian avant-garde. The cast of his mind was not derivative, the quality of his thought never second-hand. Rather, our current rediscovery of the experimental activities taking place in Russia in the 20s serves to highlight Brecht's position as not that of an isolated genius of the European avant-garde, but as the brilliant representative of a wiry strand of aesthetic history. And it is within this theorising perspective that Brecht's influence on the contemporary European cinema is incalculable. Without him, it is doubtful whether Godard, Makavejev, Straub, to mention only the most luminous figures of the radical cinematic avant-garde of today, could have produced the body of work that they have.

«Kuhle Wampe»

This article originally appeared in *Sight and Sound*, Autumn 1974, and is reproduced here by kind permission with only minor alterations.

The Political Joke in «Happiness»

Aleksandr Medvedkin. The Soviet Union, 1943. A film called *Happiness*. A gap, an absence in film histories, whether of «silent cinema», «political cinema» or «film comedy». An absence that today, on seeing *Happiness* in the context of Eisenstein and Vertov's work of that period, and in the light of the more recent explorations of Godard and Makavejev and others, seems astonishing. For the issues this film engages with are ones crucial to the debates of the past ten years as to potentially effective modes of leftist film-making. Medvedkin attacks the problem of producing entertaining films that simultaneously orient a mass audience toward a socialist future, yet without falling into the traps of «illusionism» that the socialist realists were espousing even at the moment of *Happiness* (originally entitled *Snatchers*). In this respect Medvedkin's endeavours are to be seen alongside those of Eisenstein and Vertov, though *Happiness* in no way produces a cinematic experience isomorphic to those of his two compatriots; rather, we find three very different ways in which the cinema has been inscribed within a revolutionary context. Why, then, is it only now that it is possible to make this recognition?

Film historians, it might be remarked, have a habit of uncovering «lost masterpieces» — films, most often, that simply got submerged in the mass of «product» of their time and have lain unnoticed in crammed vaults until their triumphant dusting off . . . *Happiness*, however, offers a rather special case. The whole principle of its production differs from that of most «rediscoveries». For *Happiness* was made for a specific audience at a specific moment in Soviet history; it was not aimed primarily at even a general Soviet audience, but at a rural proletariat in the midst of the attempt to make collective farms work. Unlike Eisenstein's *October* or Vertov's *Three Songs of Lenin*, which were both commissioned as national monuments, Medvedkin's film grew directly out of his local experiences on the cine-train between 1931–2.

As the French director Chris Marker (who discovered *Happiness* in the Belgian Archive in 1967) has pointed out (Marker, 1971, p.4), Jay Leyda is the only historian or critic to have mentioned the enterprise undertaken by the cine-train in 1930. This train differed markedly from its predecessors — the agit-trains of civil-war days, which carried poets and painters, state officials and films to remote areas of the country. For the 1932 train which Medvedkin led did not just take prefabricated objects into the countryside, but was instead a fully equipped film laboratory.

> *The film-train was made up of three railway cars, the first carrying living and dining quarters for a crew of thirty-two persons, the second a projection room, storage for apparatus, and a complete installation for producing animated cartoons: the third car was filled with laboratory and film-printing machinery. Pulled and tended by the railway system, this was a self-contained film studio that could maintain itself on location for months at a time without requiring supplies or even communications from a central base.* (Leyda, 1960, p.286)

Its function?

> *In addition to making instructional films to help local problems, for example overcoming winter conditions to speed up freight shipments, the film crew was also to produce critical films on local conditions (bureaucracy, inefficiency, nepotism, etc.) that they or the local political workers judged to require their ungentle attentions. The prime audience for these, as for the instructional films, was the local one ... Out of all these hasty productions some were to be chosen for national distribution.* (ibid., p.287)

In this fundamental engagement with the urgent political necessities of the time, Medvedkin's group situates itself clearly in the vanguard of cinematic thinking; at the same time, this context is clearly one that is far from the ideology of production constituted by the majority of the films that trace the supposed boundaries of film-art/film-history. The films of the cine-train were, in short, unlikely to attract attention beyond Soviet borders, even if they *did* succeed in gaining national distribution. Consequently and typically, none of these films appears to be extant today. *Happiness,* however, which was a *result* of the cine-train experience (not a product of the train itself) has survived ... but unnoticed, largely, one suspects, because of its concern with a «local» problem, that of collectives.

Except, however, that there are other compelling reasons why the film was not brandished abroad: reasons not unrelated to those which cut Vertov's experimental freedom after 1930, to those which kept Eisenstein out of the studio for so much of his life after 1930, to those which led to Meyerhold's assassination in 1940 and his subsequent elimination from Soviet theatre history. The tale of Medvedkin's career after *Happiness* is its own evidence: 1936 saw the release of another comedy, *The Miracle Girl*; 1938 saw the completion of *The New Moscow,* which was banned/not released on account of the fact that the abrasive satiric style that Medvedkin had worked on since his days in the cavalry in the twenties (when he put on theatrical shows) proved too much for the approval committees. His infrequent work of the next twenty years displays, by all accounts, none of the incisive wit and materialist vigour of *Happiness*. In fact, given what had already happened to Eisenstein's and Vertov's films by 1934, it is surprising that *Happiness* got to be released at all. For as I shall demonstrate, its visual organisation, its approach to representation, is quite at odds with the prevailing aesthetic climate of the time, even if it marks a striking congruence with those of the avant-garde of the previous decade, particularly the avant-garde at whose centre lies Meyerhold, an avant-garde whose principles were to be echoed and rigorously articulated in the work of Brecht. For by 1934 the era of experimentation in the arts in Soviet Russia was over. The Central Committee's 1932 Decree on the Reconstruction of Literary and Artistic Organisations (which had the effect of dissolving all official art groups, and the very periodicals, such as Lef, October, AKhRR*, that had nurtured the fervent debates of the twenties) proclaimed

> . . . *the confines of the existing proletarian literature and art organisations are becoming too narrow and are hampering the serious development of artistic creation.* [*They are in danger of becoming*] *an instrument for cultivating élitist withdrawal and loss of contact with the political tasks of contemporaneity* . . . (Vaughan James, 1973, p. 120)

This was followed in 1934 by the first All-Union Congress of Soviet Writers, chaired by Maxim Gorky, which advocated «socialist realism» as the *only* viable aesthetic. (As someone puts it in *Vent d'est* [Wind from the East], made, indeed, by the Dziga Vertov Group led by Godard and Gorin: «the most disgusting aspect of the cinema is that the bourgeoisie and Stalin have the same attitude».) It was at this conference that Zhdanov announced «. . . the Socialist way of life has gained *final* and *complete* victory in our country — under the leadership of the Communist Party and under our leader of genius, Comrade Stalin.»** Attitudes such as this increasingly overwhelmed Meyerhold's urgent plea of four years earlier: «The audience of today must be

---

*Assotsiatsiya Khudozhnikov Revolutsionnoi Rossii (Association of Revolutionary Russian Artists) 1922-3.
**Pervy vsesoyuzny s'ezd sovetskykh pisatelei (stenograficheskhy otchet): First Pan-Union Session of Soviet Writers (transcript).

shocked into realising that there are battles still to be won, that the time is not yet ripe for a summing-up.» (Meyerhold, 1969) The concept of perpetual revolution, so central both to Marx and to avant-garde aesthetic theory, was due for a rough time. It was not surprising that the comic inventiveness of Medvedkin was suppressed. But as far as *Happiness'* place in film history is concerned, there is a third reason that explains its absence: it was the last silent film made in Russia at a time when Soviet film production was concentrating on sound. Most histories are geared to «firsts», not «lasts».

The moment of *Happiness'* rediscovery came, appropriately, in France in the late sixties as a significant section of France's intellectuals began to search for an appropriate mode of relating political work and aesthetic activities. This search was particularly concentrated in film, and two groups specifically oriented themselves toward the Soviet precedents. On the one hand there was Godard and Gorin's formation of the Dziga Vertov group, and on the other, Chris Marker's foundation, two years earlier, of SLON, a co-operative film group dedicated to exploring various ways of working outside the film industry. SLON made films about workers' problems, about international problems (*The Battle of the Ten Million*); they produced a film «magazine», and rediscovered *Happiness* and the name of Medvedkin in the Belgian Cinémathèque. This rediscovery was clearly important to the group: not only did they prepare *Happiness* for distribution again, they also made a half-hour film, *The Train Rolls On* about the cine-train experience, which included a long interview with Medvedkin himself. Marker, Godard and others also formed in December 1967 a «Medvedkin Group», with Godard lending his Super-8 to the workers in the Rhodiacéta factory near Lyons. And there is even a cryptic allusion to *Happiness* in the hairdressing sequence of *Deux ou trois choses que je sais d'elle.*

The fact remains, however, that SLON's primary interest in Medvedkin lies in the notion of collective work demonstrated by the cine-trains, in the working method of that agitational enterprise. The same must be said of Leyda's account, which casts provocative allusions suggesting the lineage of Medvedkin's comic practice. He mentions Medvedkin's connection with Okhlopkov, a man who quit film directing in 1928, when his third film, *Way of the Enthusiasts,* was denied release by the authorities. Okhlopkov had apparently trained in Meyerhold's bio-mechanics class — and in the thirties there were to be a number of hostile exchanges between the two men on matters of theatrical practice. *Way of the Enthusiasts* attracted «intriguing accusations of its attempt to apply Eisenstein's ‹intellectual› methods to comedy problems» (Leyda, op. cit., p. 174). Leyda then describes Medvedkin as «a worthy heir» of Okhlopkov and Sennett. Tantalisingly this both suggests Medvedkin's situation within the avant-garde debates of the period, and also warns us not to try and place him *simply* within a Meyerholdian tradition.

Similarly, the recent resuscitation of interest in Brecht's praxis could easily lead to a claiming of Medvedkin for the Brechtian cause. This is not my interest, though it is *from* an interest in Brecht and the problems he poses for cinematic practice that my interest in Medvedkin arose. For one thing, the theoretical affinities (there is no causal link) between Brecht and Meyerhold are considerable, and Medvedkin's *Happiness* does seem to offer an instance of a film which adopts, coincidentally or not, a number of positions – representational processes – close to those explored by Meyerhold and Brecht. For this reason, given the paucity of the «Brechtian tradition» in cinema, it is of considerable interest.

Happiness constitutes a specific moment, a point of juncture of various lines of force, thought, practice. There are aspects of the second half of the film that might explain its acceptance by the socialist realists, for instance, just as, doubtless, the film should be placed within the tradition of Soviet Comedy practised by Kuleshov, Popov, Barnet, and Protazanov. It is in full awareness of the claims of these alternative perspectives that I am, nevertheless, going to consider *Happiness* specifically in terms of its relation to Meyerhold and Brecht, its transformation of certain of their hypotheses to a cinematic arena. Leyda points towards the terms of this relation when he writes with reticent understatement of its «slightly theatrical air about sets and costumes» (op. cit., p.327). For this «theatrical» element is constantly posed against the naturalising thrust of the moving-picture image, effecting in film terms what Brecht suggested had to be done for the still-photograph – it had to be literarised, captioned. Every episode of *Happiness* in the first half of the film is marked by strategies that persistently interrupt, divert any tendency towards a naturalist/realist *mise en scène*. These strategies are quite diverse, ranging from the film's episodic organisation to its use of actors, from its representation of objects to its editing principles, and it is clear that Medvedkin's approach to cinematic vision is concerned with political decisions that operate at every level of articulation in *Happiness*.

Chris Marker's interest has already isolated the political significance of Medvedkin's work in terms of its mode of production, marking its notion of aesthetic activity as a form of labour. As Bogdanov put it in 1920:

> *Creation, whether technological, socio-economic, political, domestic, scientific or artistic, represents a kind of* labour *and, like labour, is composed of organisational (or disorganisational) human endeavours.* (1924, p.192)*

We may understand this more precisely through reference to Walter Benjamin's 1934 lecture, «The Author as Producer», in which he underlines Brecht's call to avoid

---

*In a speech, «The Paths of Proletarian Creativity», delivered to the All-Russia Congress of Proletkult organisations, 1920.

> . . . *simply transmit[ting] the apparatus of production without similtaneously changing it to the maximum extent possible in the direction of socialism.* (Benjamin, 1970, p.93)

And he quotes Brecht as writing:

> . . . *certain works should no longer so much relate individual experiences (have the character of a work), but rather should be aimed at the utilisation (transformation) of certain institutes or institutions.* (ibid.)

This also echoes Bogdanov:

> *The old artist sees the revelation of his individuality in his work; the new artist will understand and feel that within his work and through his work he is creating a grand totality: collectivism . . . The old artist need or need not value artistic clarity; for the new artist, this means nothing less than collective accessibility, and this contains the vital meaning of the artist's endeavour.* (op. cit., p.197)

There is, of course, a shifting focus through these quotations — from collective work to collective accessibility of, in Medvedkin's case, a message about collectives.

Happiness is a film whose basic priority is that of clarity. Keeping the intended audience firmly in mind (a rural proletariat of only partial literacy), clarity is the key to all of Medvedkin's devices (in opposition, it could be asserted, to some of Eisenstein's work). The politics of its representational strategies achieve their materialist impact from the very simplicity of their anti-naturalist conception.

Medvedkin transforms Mayakovsky's dictum that «the theatre is not a magnifying glass, but a distorting mirror» by refusing to photograph any «pre-existing reality», opting instead to construct a representation consisting of only those elements germane to his themes. The combination of these elements is never represented as a direct «reflection of reality», but as an allegorical distortion. In brief, his images are presented explicitly as signifying practice. Thus, for instance, his hyperbolic use of objects such as chains, padlocks, and the grotesquely twisted tree that serves also as a schematic sign of the film's geographic space; or, differently, tilting the camera to accentuate the steepness of the hill that the horse and Khmyr try to plough — all these devices establish the scenes as being constructed and not reflective of the real world «out there». The scene thus hovers between the dual presence of signifier (the tilted frame) and signified (the difficulty of ploughing a steep hill). This play between the two terms has, as we shall see shortly, important repercussions for the efficacy of Medvedkin's comic technique. And the way this sequence evolves demonstrates well Medvedkin's theatrical rather than realist *mise en scène,* particularly in its disregard for the illusionist transitions between shots, which transitions normally have as one co-ordinate of their functioning to guarantee the «real» space of the actions. The sequence culminates in the horse's death when it is instantly purged from the frame (no corpse to «realistically» litter the screen): it is neither removed by anyone, nor yet present – except in so far as Anna «his horsewife» replaces, reconstitutes the beast in harness. Once this metaphor is established, the horse is re-introduced in frame, resurrected, in a shot of it sitting, cat-like, on its hind legs. The placing of this shot situates the horse as a cynical onlooker, as it were, from the wings of this theatrical space and the very act of resurrection effectively blocks any naturalist reading of the scene.

Again and again through the film Medvedkin constructs images whose metaphoric function overrides their naturalist function: the nuns in transparent blouses (down whose bodies the camera tilts lasciviously) represent unequivocally the church's degradation, its prostitution to the desires of the military. Or take the later scene in which one of the collective is seduced by Foka's trap of a bottle of vodka (Fig. 1) – the spiritual encirclement, captivation, is represented directly in visual terms, the idea becomes image. In another scene (Fig. 2) Khmyr's lassitude is shown as infectious – his horse too (constantly endowed with human characteristics) is falling asleep, the frame's internal rhyming effect clinching both the humorous and didactic elements of the scene. The previous shot has been of water draining out of the barrel behind Khmyr, following a title that Khmyr is «losing all faith in happiness» – the process of loss being represented by the water trickling away down the hill. The *economy* of these images is crucial to the functioning of their comic articulation, as we shall shortly see more clearly. Similarly, in Fig. 3, the image of the granary on legs is a remarkable visualisation of the *effect* of robbers, a surrealist heightening of their basic activity, and again it is the *economy* of the representation that is fundamental, as is true, in an earlier scene, of the gate with a fence on only one side, where the economy of the visual wit consists in playing the conventional meaning against itself – the *meaning* of fences, i.e. possessiveness, territoriality, against its actual lack.

At this point let me quote Meyerhold, in a lecture on «Chaplin and Chaplinism»:

> Let us go to our children and see how naïvely they draw, yet what great art they produce. Eisenstein tells an interesting story of a child illustrating the subject «lighting the stove». The child drew «some firewood, a stove, and a chimney. But in the middle of the room there was a huge rectangle covered with zig-zags. What was it? Matches apparently. The child drew the matches on a scale appropriate to their crucial role in the action he was depicting.» (op. cit., pp.320–1)

It is immediately clear that this observation of a child's representation of

Fig 1

Fig 2   *Fig 3*

«lighting the stove» illuminates elements of Medvedkin's mode of representation (padlocks, chains etc); but it has, I think, rather profounder implications for our comprehension of the film's mechanisms. Freud, in *Jokes and their Relation to the Unconscious,* isolates two fundamental principles from which «all the techniques of jokes, and accordingly all pleasure from these techniques, are derived» (Freud, 1905, p. 127). These two principles are firstly, «economising in psychical expenditure that is only about to be called for»; secondly, and more to our purpose here, «relief from psychical expenditure that is already there», or as Freud himself paraphrases it, «re-establishing old liberties and getting rid of the burden of intellectual upbringing.» The return to a former state, i.e. analagous to childhood, Freud finds to be a basic operation in the functioning of jokes. Indeed, in constructing his model for the functioning of jokes, Freud poses a three-stage movement, play→jest→joke, in which the first stage is explicitly a child-like activity:

> *Play appears in children while they are learning to make use of words and to put thoughts together. This play probably obeys one of the instincts which compel children to practise their capacities. Play with words and thoughts, motivated by certain pleasurable effects of economy, would thus be the first stage of jokes.* (ibid., p. 128)

The second stage is «the jest», which

> *. . . is a question of prolonging the yield of pleasure from play, but at the same time of silencing the objections raised by criticism which would not allow the pleasurable*

feeling to emerge. There is only one way of reaching this end: the meaningless combination of words or the absurd putting together of thoughts must nevertheless have a meaning. (ibid., p. 129)

The third stage is only relatively different from the second: «If what a jest says possesses substance and value [as opposed to being merely «permissible»], it turns into a joke.» (ibid., p. 131) Now in the first section of *Jokes and their Relation to the Unconscious*, Freud suggests that there are both «innocent» and «tendentious» jokes, only the latter having a target, the former existing merely for the pleasure of «play». However, he later comes to realise that:

Jokes, even if the thought contained in them is non-tendentious, and thus only serves theoretical intellectual interests, are in fact never non-tendentious. . . . A joke is a psychical factor possessed of power: its weight, thrown into one scale or the other, can be decisive. (ibid., pp. 132–3)

Joking, then, is never simply a question of «entertainment», of «mere fun», and Medvedkin grasps this, and it is possible – if we may transfer some of Freud's observations on verbal jokes to the rather different area of film – to see how he uses comedy to produce his «collectivisation» message.

Instead of arguing his case for collectivisation, or against the clergy, in a solemn, studied manner (much as Eisenstein attempts in *October*), Medvedkin exploits the psychical powers of joking to orientate his audience to their socialist future. Freud, in coming to his principle of «relief from psychical expenditure that is already there», arrived via two categories of jokes: one he calls «replacement of thing-associations by word-association», by which he means what we would now call the shifting of the focus of attention from the signified to the signifier; the other revolves around the «use of absurdity». Both these forms can be seen to operate in *Happiness*.

In one group of . . . jokes (play upon words) the technique consisted in focusing our psychical attitude upon the sound of the word instead of upon its meaning – in making the (acoustic) word-presentation itself take the place of its significance as given by its relations to thing-presentations. It may really be suspected that in doing so we are bringing about a great relief in psychical work, and that when we make serious use of words we are obliged to hold ourselves back with a certain effort from this comfortable procedure. (Freud, op. cit., p. 119)

Happiness demonstrates the transformation of this technique into filmic terms, while maintaining the recognition that the fundamental shift specified by Freud occurs between signified and signifier. Many of the gags are predicated on the deliberate foregrounding of filmic articulations: the use of high-speed movement (a camera «deviation» from the norm), the use of superimposition

(Foka's «magical» appearance on the hillside), of animation techniques (*vareneki* – little cakes – «flying» unaided into Foka's mouth), are all used to make points. But our acceptance of them is rooted, not in a belief in the authenticity of the representation, but in our acknowledgment of the witty appositeness of that representation *as* representation. Let's examine one sequence in some detail: the fight on the bridge between the tall and short clergymen. The scene has been set: the two have already found a five kopeck* piece on the road, and have each outdone the other in their ingratiating attempts to make their companion accept the pittance. Then a purse of gold is espied on a bridge, their «real» characters emerge (Medvedkin's original title for the film was *Snatchers*) and they fight for the booty. Medvedkin doesn't just set his actors to fighting – instead he utilises purely filmic capacities to *abstract* the fight from any spatio-temporal coherence, using a series of jump-cuts to fragment the continuity, and accentuate the crazy, frenzied quality of the aggression. Figs. 4–9 are from this sequence, 4/5 being adjacent frames, as are also 6/7 and 8/9. As can instantly be seen, there is no logical continuity within the pairs, no logic of character placement within the frame; nor (as is not evident from stills) is there any attempt to match the direction of movement from one shot to the next. In fact the principal logic of this sequence is non-narrative: Medvedkin concentrates on the rhythm of the sequence, both in the length of each shot, and on the alternating angle of orientation of the camera. Shots 4, 5, 6 have a perspective receding from right to left, while 7, 8, 9 recede from left to right. This formal play (the alternating perspectives have no narrative or identificatory function) establishes a distinctly non-naturalist space – particularly since one of the priests seems constantly in the air, the jump-cuts eliding portions where he might touch the ground. In short, Medvedkin does not attempt to convince us of the animal greed of the clergy by demonstrating a seriously mean and bloody struggle – but by focusing on the material articulations of the celluloid, by concentrating on the rhythmic and abstract spatial logic of the representation of the fight, he denudes the clergy of any dignity, integrity: the conventional, socialised meanings of «priesthood» are left utterly stranded. By working on a kind of primal pleasure of the play with filmic elements, instead of with «responsible» analysis of the hypocrisy and greed of the church (which analysis would, in classical narrative, involve the effacement of the signifying process), Medvedkin reintroduces a certain materiality of language, and through the play on that material, pulls the spectator onto his side through the force of agreement engendered by the pleasurable effect.

> A *cheerful mood, whether it is produced endogenously or toxically, reduces the inhibiting forces, criticism among them, and makes accessible once again sources of pleasure which were under the weight of suppression.* (Freud, op. cit., p.127)

*Soviet socialist realism was widely known as «an art for five kopecks».

In so far as *Happiness* is concerned, Medvedkin's targets of religion, the Tsarist military, state functionaries and so on, are prime institutional instances of psychical pressure upon his audience – pressures that persisted in 1934. (As Meyerhold pointed out in 1930, «There are 36,805 religious organisations in the RSFSR*. The total of religious communities has almost doubled since

Fig 4

Fig 5

Fig 6

Fig 7

Fig 8

Fig 9

1922–3.» (op. cit.)) Ridiculing all notions of paternalistic and spiritual authority throughout the first half of *Happiness,* Medvedkin contrives in the second to leave traces of that authority, which are finally overwhelmed by the imperatives of collectivist commitment. These traces are constituted by the successive reappearences of the same actors who play, for instance, the clergy of the bridge fight – this Laurel and Hardy duo also appears as robbers and as

*Russian Soviet Federal Socialist Republic.

anti-collective subversives. The multi-role system endows each successive appearance with an accumulated force of rejection, sets up a trail of metaphorical accretions that spread through the film. On the one hand (recalling Meyerhold's *Give Us Europe* of 1924, in which 95 roles were played by 45 players) the multiple roles played by each actor (except Khmyr, Anna and Foka) function to remind us that, as Brecht put it «the actor is quoting»: certainly there is an underlining of the dual personality of the actor, growing perhaps out of Meyerhold's formula $N = A_1 + A_2$ (where N is the actor, A_1 is the artist who conceives the idea and issues the instructions necessary for its execution, and A_2 is the executant who executes the conception of A); in short a materialist notion of the actor, as opposed to one of the actor as «a man possessed» by his role. On the other hand, we must clearly read the succession of roles offered by each actor as also shaping a historical sequence, that of the rise and fall of the church, but this historical sequence is realised, temporally, in very schematic terms. Despite the perhaps thirty-five year time-span of *Happiness'* narrative, no-one ages in this film: the actor quotes, he does not «live through» the events re-presented.

At this point let me return to the fight on the bridge: apart from Medvedkin's handling of the editing of the sequence, and the spatial and temporal discontinuities of the fight, there is also the actors' representation of the fight to be considered. (And it should be considered from the point of view of Brecht's emphasis on the necessity of «the gest», of gestic acting, an emphasis prefigured in Meyerhold's statement that «every movement is a hieroglyph with its own peculiar meaning».) There is no attempt to convince us these are *real* blows; instead a blow-by-blow mime is played out, one priest *waiting* to be hit on the head by a (pathetically thin) stick, then the postures switch, as the other priest *waits* to be punched in the stomach, this «stagey» blow-taking has devastating effect: the key-note is absurdity. The absurdity has two distinct functions: to ridicule (like Sennett), and also to emphasise the materialist basis of this representation, developing the spectator's critical, scrutinising activity. Near the end of the bridge sequence, the short priest is left alone, alternately peering into the water after his companion, and over his shoulder for the purse. Medvedkin elides the space between these two gazes, endowing the man with preposterous, owl-like swiftness, the rapid alternation between these two looks working both to deflate what little may be left of the priest's dignity, and to reinforce the material articulations of the filmic discourse. There is an interesting connection to be made here between the conventions of priesthood (i.e. its socialised meanings), and the naturalising conventions of cinematic language. Freud has noted that:

> *Nothing distinguishes jokes more clearly from all other psychical structures than this double-sidedness and this duplicity in speech. From this point of view at least, the authorities come closest to an understanding of the nature of jokes when they lay stress*

on *«sense in nonsense»*. (Freud, op. cit., p. 172)

The priesthood is here mocked through Medvedkin's play upon the elements underpinning the visual representation of priesthood. In sum, we may say that the whole bridge sequence is organised through a play of formal elements, which play undergoes a process of transformation onto the level of content. This process corresponds to that moment in Freud's model of the operation of jokes, in which «the meaningless combination of words or the absurd putting-together of thoughts is found nevertheless to have a meaning». The «nonsensical» fight takes on meaning, is transferred to the character of the priests.

It is important, of course, that this transfer is of a very generalised meaning, pertaining not to the *individual* priest(s), but to the ideological structures that inform their roles. Indeed Medvedkin meticulously avoids any individualising tendency in his presentation of all the «enemies» of collectivisation. Even Foka, the incarnation of Tsarist evil, remains abstract, incarnating a «magical» force of evil: food flies unaided to his mouth, he appears out of the air on the hillside. Magic (the intangible, spiritual) is a weapon of Tsarist forces, and is closely related to religious superstitions: Khmyr's praying for a life of plenty must be replaced by pragmatic energy. And the representation of Khmyr is emphatically generalised: for one thing, the titles underline this — he is representative of the Russian peasant class, *he* must feed Russia, *he* «was shipped 3 and 30 years, was shot on 12 fronts and whipped 7 times in the Carpathians». This generalising thrust recurs in a somewhat different form in Godard's *Deux ou trois choses que je sais d'elle, Weekend* and, particularly obviously, in *Vent d'est* when a single image of a woman, her face hidden by the leaves of a tree, is given four different historical identities: Suzanne Monet, Scarlett Faulkner, Ines Mussolini, Rachel Darnev, each marking a different but related manifestation of right-wing ideology. The notion of «typicality» is, of course, central to the operations of socialist realism. What differentiates Godard's and Medvedkin's generalisations from such a concept of typicality is their refusal to integrate that typicality into the flux of the «real world»: instead, as for example in the repetitions of the soldiers' grotesque masks in *Happiness,* they foreground the representation *as* signifying practice.

Happiness can be described, then, as an avant-garde film, in so far as it offers what Stephen Heath has called «a representation of the real functioning of representation». Again and again we find the representational activity in the foreground of our engagement with the film: Medvedkin seems to underline both the static and two-dimensional foundations of the cinematic process. We consistently meet a *tableau* quality that re-marks Brecht's observation that «cinema is by nature static and must be treated as a series of *tableaux*»: not merely the distinctly episodic structuring of the film's narration, but images such as the very opening shot of the film, whose immobility seems to contradict the very idea of any imminent cinematic action; or the shots of the «crescent moon» set that bracket the night-time scenes (the formally repetitive use of the crescent moon re-marks it as signifying practice). Similarly, Medvedkin's recourse to high-angle long shots (e.g. the Caligari-esque grave-yard for the scene of Anna banishing Khmyr), in which the horizon is excluded from the frame and the actors are relatively small in the image (as often in Keaton), results in an impassive, ironic stance toward the charged, even melodramatic content, takes us *out* of the action. Such a detachment makes impossible any *emotional* identification with Khmyr of Anna. The most emphatic example of this is Khmyr's fantasy (Figs. 10 and 11), which is constructed as a kind of *flattened tableau*: the first two shots of the sequence (establishing long shots) have what appears to be a diamond-patterned floor, but the perspectival implications that it holds if we consider it as floor (i.e. *horizontal*) are contradicted by the apparent matching of a diamond-shaped grid, placed *vertically* in an archway on the right of the screen. It is, in short, difficult to read the space of this fantasy as three-dimensional, and the only marginal variation of the camera's frontal/proscenium-arch position throughout the series of shots that make up the sequence reinforces, in its ignoring of the 30° rule that aids in establishing the impression of real space, this lack of perspectival conviction.

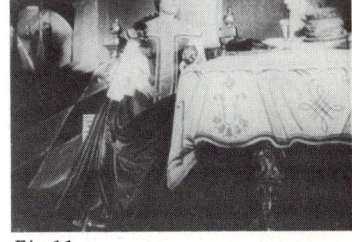

Fig 10   *Fig 11*

The lack of perspectival conviction matters in so far as it aids in Medvedkin's debunking of the folkloric origin of this fantasy — Khmyr's greasing his hair with his hands after devouring a leg of chicken, Anna's *snapping* at an apple, function to strip this embedded legend of its force, just as elsewhere Medvedkin parodies the folkwisdom that «a horse, a full granary and a house» equal Happiness. Medvedkin's use of folk-lore is similar to Brecht's interest in epic — both are well-known to their audience, thus there is no necessity for detailed itemisation of «reality», for a phenomenologically authentic representation. But Chaplin too used epic (especially *The Gold Rush*), without it being either materialist or socialist. Eisenstein saw why: «Chaplin's gag is individualist; with Medvedkin it's socialist.» (Eisenstein, 1971)* Even in

---
*The letter was written in 1936 but not published then.

Modern Times, which is still a remarkable condemnation of technological dehumanisation, there can be no doubt that Chaplin's is a transcendental humour: he rises above the «petty miseries» of the world, he transforms mechanical rhythms into inspired balletics. Chaplin criticises, satirises, but without ever analysing the *causes* of the misery he describes; for him it is enough simply to rise above it, *personally* escape it. There is certainly no interest in class-consciousness — for his worker-colleagues are as frequently comic targets as anyone else. Medvedkin has no interest in individual escapes, but rather in collective social solutions. In this Medvedkin is unique among directors of silent comedy, just as his example is extraordinary in its attempt to make comic films for a very specific and localised audience, quite unlike the universalist aspirations of a Chaplin or Keaton. The strength of Medvedkin's work derives in part from its engagement in a concrete struggle, a continuing struggle. Against Zhdanov's 1934 proclamation of a fully-achieved revolution, Medvedkin underlines the continuing infiltration of revolutionary ranks by decadent elements. With Lenin he admits that:

> *It is normal that the peasant will not come immediately to socialism. It is necessary that he verifies in practice that toward which he is called. He decides to change his life when he comprehends the necessity.* (Medvedkin, quoted in *L'Avant-Scène du Cinéma,* No. 120, December 1971)

Happiness contributes to the possibility of that comprehension, placing education with entertainment, combining pleasure with learning in the manner of Brecht's «Lehrstücke», learning-plays. For Medvedkin's use of comedy (unlike Chaplin's) is in explicit recognition of Freud's observation that all jokes have a «tendency», in this case a socialist tendency: *Happiness* represents one attempt at an answer to Meyerhold's pleas of 1930:

> *If the modern theatre [let us read «cinema»] is to justify its existence, it must not purvey some pointless commercial fiction. It must inspire the audience to leave the performance determined to tackle the construction with renewed vigour . . .*
>
> *We have already renounced the apolitical theatre . . . but who knows how to stage productions which imbue the spectator with that vigour which seems to use the best means of defending the more vulnerable elements of the population against the poison gases of the clerics and the kulaks, against the decadent opiates of the urban bourgeoisie?* (op. cit., p.268)

Medvedkin has, at least, some suggestions.

This article appeared in *Screen,* Vol. 19, No. 1, Spring 1978, and is republished here by kind permission, restored to its original, longer version. We have indicated those references we have been able to locate during the preparation of this anthology.

Political Formations in the Cinema of Jean-Marie Straub

Few North American film-makers and critics have approached political cinema with the radically conceived theoretical foundations that may be seen in a number of their European counterparts, and this difference of approach is currently foregrounded in the hostility toward the films of Frenchman Jean-Marie Straub.* His works are rarely exhibited, even in festivals, and yet they have acquired a formidable reputation for opacity and tedium. The reasons for this response are not difficult to comprehend, since they lie within the boundaries of a debate over the constitutive elements of political art, a debate which has, even today, barely emerged into the public forum in North America. That is to say, since the Cubist painters, since Eisenstein and Vertov in the cinema, since Meyerhold and Brecht in the theatre, the central problematic of radical art has been the extent to which the *form* of the art-work must be radical, in support of its content. It is suggested that a work of art can *only* be radical if its articulating structure is as subversive of conventional forms as its «content» is critical of the dominant ideology.

This attitude is, clearly, not at one with our experience of much «political» film thought in the USA. For the «radical» films that are most widely acclaimed — *Battle of Algiers, Z, The Ballad of Joe Hill* — are all characterised by the very devices whose validity Straub (and Godard) consistently deny. While Pontecorvo, Costa-Gavras and Widerberg construct their various discourses around the emotional susceptibilities of the viewer, through the melodramatic conventions of identification procedures (antipathy towards the thugs of *Z*, empathy for the nobely *humane* Joe Hill). Straub has rejected this approach, attacking instead through the intellectual paths suggested by a thorough and critical examination of the conventional assumptions of both film industry and audience.

Where many American radicals appear to operate on the level of substituting anti-bourgeois/proletarian/materialist content for the bourgeois/imperial/capitalist content of the Hollywood product, a few of their European counterparts can be seen working out of a more generalised notion of revolt. For these European directors, the Hollywood film (now perceived as a *global*

---

*Although French by birth, much of his life has been spent under German influence (German-occupied France during the war, and then ten years living in Munich from 1958), and several of his films reveal an absorption in the nature of the German psyche of the post-war years.

form – Brezhnev/Mosfilm – Nixon/Paramount, as Godard puts it) is merely the most recent manifestation of illusionism. Perspectival oil painting and the nineteenth-century novel in particular established certain codes which came to be accepted as prerequisite for filmic expression. In the first twenty years or so of its life, the cinema gradually adapted to conform to these traditional codes of expression; this process or adaptation is particularly clear in D. W. Griffith's work between 1908 and 1913, in which we find, for instance, an increasing dependence on the apparent *depth* of the image to «prove» its «reality»; or, again, the development of an editing style which wouldn't rupture either the

Huillet and Straub

spectator's identification with the characters on the screen, or his/her sense of the narrative's *continuity:* thus the «180° rule», and the use of «shot/reverse shot» cutting become entrenched as elements of *the* way of making cinematic narratives.*

---

*The 180° rule in cinematography means that the camera can point from anywhere at the subject so long as the camera is positioned only on one side of an imaginary line traced along the course of the subject's movement or along the line of the subject's glance. This guarantees that the person's glance or movement will seem to be in the same direction from shot to shot, and that any change in direction of glance or movement will occur according to narrative exigency and not because the camera was placed on opposite sides of the subject in successive shots. It is a rule observed in shooting so that the footage can be edited «logically» together. If the rule is broken, a person might be walking from left to right in one shot, but would appear to be walking from right to left in the next – with no indication of having turned.

«Shot/reverse shot» cutting is called by the French *champ-contre-champ,* and very simply refers to showing the subject against a certain background and then cutting to a shot of that subject filmed *from* that background.

Brecht's initial elaboration of his theories of epic theatre, and the slightly earlier work of Eisenstein and Vertov, together form the first prong of a politically motivated attack on this «illusionist» tradition. According to Brecht (and subsequently to Walter Benjamin), the radical work of art must oppose the illusionist mode at *every* level. Thus the means of expression is itself called into question: because the «means of expression» are ideologically determined it is no longer sufficient to place a new «content» within the old structures of expression. Instead, the signifying system itself must be attacked, in order to overthrow the basis upon which the dominant ideological message rests. This procedure constitutes the crux of Godard's work, particularly since 1968, and it lies similarly embedded in the films of Jean-Marie Straub: much of his work may be elucidated in terms of a systematic «deconstruction» of the old forms of cinematic expression.

One film in which the notion of «deconstruction» may be seen with particularly clarity is Straub's *Eyes do not want to close at all times, or perhaps one day Rome will permit herself to choose in her turn*, usually referred to as *Othon* (1970, 83 minutes). The basis of the film is a performance of Corneille's play, *Othon* — but it is a performance which integrates the *circumstances* of that performance, and the process of its transformation into film, into its totality as an aesthetic object. That is to say, where an illusionist director would have simply created an historical melodrama, an autonomous world into which we would be transported for the duration of the film, Straub commences his film by presenting only a rear-view of the actors, concentrating our attention on Rome's rush-hour traffic in the background. Then the camera moves in to the actors who deliver their lines rapidly, in a kind of expressive monotone: monotone because each character/actor hardly varies his style or pace of delivery, expressive because each monotone differs from the others, and suggests certain formalised relationships *vis-à-vis* the other characters. For instance, Galba, the old emperor, always paces his speech very slowly, and this dignity emphasises his position at the head of his social hierarchy. The message is clear, but the signifier of that message is equally so, in its formalised conception. Straub doesn't try to present either speech or gesture as naturalistic, but heightens their formalisations, thus conforming to Brecht's dictum: «Instead of wanting to create the impression that he is improvising, the actor should rather show what the truth is: he is quoting.»

Perhaps the most radical aspect of Straub's *Othon*, however, is his use of cutting and framing, both of which are designed in opposition to the illusionist codes of representation, and serve to eliminate the possibility of any identification with the characters. Frequently cuts are made apparently arbitrarily, instead of conforming to some psychological demand; on other occasions, Straub violates the 180° rule, emphasising the shot's materiality, rather than its transparence. The camera, in an illusionst film, is subordinated to the movements of the central dramatic characters — it pans to follow their motion, it moves to a close-up to record moments of «intensity»; Straub's camera never pans to follow movement, but follows a logic of its own, a logic devoted to the articulation of the material space in which the action takes place. The play is not the central discourse, which the images illustrate in a servile manner. In this connection, Noël Burch recently observed:

> *The idea that there are two tracks — an image-track and a sound-track — is something that people are not even remotely aware of in any sense, and therefore are not aware of the fact that essentially these are two different productions happening . . . the dominant concept is that the image produces the sound.* (Burch, 1974, p.30)*

Othon's opening shot, which contains modern houses, and the ruins on the Palatine Hill, but no people, hints at the dislocation between «image-track» and «sound-track» that is to recur through the film; for instance, Straub often refrains from giving us an establishing shot at the beginning of a sequence: thus we don't know *who* is being spoken to, or even, on occasion, who is speaking, until the end of the sequence.

This decentralisation of the actors is constant through the film, both in their frequent partial framing, and Straub's use of the «empty» frame.† Where the illusionist film centres its lead actors in the frame, Straub does not: in the sequence by the fountain, Vinius enters, and is initially seen only from the waist down, until he sits by Plautine, and when the camera subsequently shifts in on Plautine, Vinius is bisected by the left side of the screen — precisely the opposite of what the laws of «good photography» allow. (Similarly, the sound of the fountain is allowed to dominate the soundtrack, partially displacing the conventional centre of aural attention, the text of the play.) And where the illusionist film cuts when a character exits from the frame (in order to expedite the progress of the narrative) Straub frequently lets his camera rest for twenty or thirty seconds on the «empty» screen: the materiality of the space in which the characters operate is reasserted. Further — and this is essential to the practical aesthetic success of Straub's project, as opposed to the veracity of his theoretical intentions — these «empty» spaces take on a rhythmic function, become a mode of punctuation, since their most emphatic occurrences coincide with the end of an act in Corneille's text. Indeed this rhythmic aspect is one which it is virtually impossible to perceive in the sub-titled prints of the film, since one devotes so much time to reading that the aural music of

---

*Elsewhere in this interview Burch elaborates the notion of «deconstruction» rather more fully than is possible here.

†I am partly indebted to Beverly Alcock for this observation; a more detailed analysis of *Othon* as a «deconstruction» film may be found in her thesis (for the Slade Film Department, University College, London) entitled «An Introduction to Some of the Problems Produced by Work on the Notion of Readership, and the Concept of a Materialist Practice in the Field of Film».

Corneille's verse (which is magnificently highlighted by its formalised delivery) passes by almost unnoticed.

Inevitably, new ways of thinking are more difficult to adapt to than simply «new contents» expressed through the same fundamental method of expression as the «old content». And that Straub's films are *difficult* remains unquestionable — but the hostility that has greeted them is due rather to the audience's lack of a critical framework within which to situate them, than to any mindless incompetence on Straub's part. Straub's films are certainly not populist in any sense, but the fact that they appeal only to a small audience is not, surely, a critical stigma. (Nor is it an automatic accolade!) For what then of Dreyer, Snow, post- '68 Godard — or of Stockhausen, Cage, Reich, Varèse, in music?

«Othon»

What we have to accept as a given at this point is the idea that significant political activity (as well as aesthetic activity) can take place on the level of intellectual theory, even though this may result in a comparatively rarefied practice. This obviously involves a broadening of the commonly held idea that politics is a pragmatic activity directed toward social manipulation. And here Godard's distinction between «making a political film» and «making a film politically» is of crucial importance. For, as Roland Barthes remarked apropos of Brecht:

Capitalist society endures, and communism itself is being transformed: revolutionary action must increasingly cohabit, and in almost institutional fashion, with the norms of bourgeois and petit-bourgeois morality: problems of conduct, and no longer of action, arise. (Barthes, 1972 p.75; emphasis by M.W.)

[. . .] Of course Godard's distinction applies equally to viewing films: just as there is no guarantee that we view political films politically, so we may view non-political films in a political manner (cf. the article by Chuck Kleinhans in *Jump Cut* no. 2, 1974).

Straub's films are not merely complexly conceived in themselves, they demand considerable mental activity on the part of the audience. [. . .] As Peter Wollen has remarked apropos of *Vent d'est,* we ask «What is this film for», rather than merely internal questions such as «What is going to happen next?» (Wollen, 1972) In order to gain anything from viewing a film by Straub, the viewer is forced to work at the production of meaning. [. . .] In a sense, it is a process of co-creation between Straub and his audience, there is no trace of paternalistic condescension: he feeds us no easy answers.

In the demands he makes on his audience, in his rigorous analysis of the syntax of his medium of expression, as well as in his broad notion of what constitutes political activity, Straub is clearly very close to the spirit of Godard. Indeed we may say that in many respects Straub's work *parallels* Godard's continuing investigation of the potential strengths and limitations of the film medium, and the two directors have expressed their mutual admiration (Godard helped finance *The Chronicle of Anna Magdalena Bach,* 1968, 93 minutes). But in artistic temperament and moral sensibility, Straub recalls the work of Rossellini: in both, we might cite reflection, analysis, documentarism as their core qualities. Both refuse to manipulate or exploit their material for emotional ends. In each it is the precise integrity of the director's analytic powers that renders his work political, in its profoundest, moral sense: political in the manner they assume a responsibility to their subject matter. This responsibility is succinctly (and amusingly) suggested by the anecdote of Rossellini berating his cameraman for removing a boulder from the foreground of a landscape they were filming, saying that if nature put it there, art has no business removing it. Similarly André Bazin wrote of Rossellini that «Man himself is just one fact among others, to whom no pride of place should be given *a priori*» (Bazin, 1971, p.38), thereby pointing to a sensibility we find recurring in Straub's films, in such things as his insistence on using direct sound rather than post-synchronisation, and his refusal to «type» actors according to convictions that demand «good» characters be handsome, «bad» ones visibly meretricious, and so on.

This latter refusal was in part responsible for the hostility that his first film, *Machorka-Muff* (1963, 17 minutes) provoked. Adapted from Heinrich Böll's magazine story, «Bonn Diary», it told of the visit of Colonel Machorka-Muff to Bonn, to visit his mistress, and clear the name of General Hurlanger-Hiss, who had been accused of retreating in battle after losing only 8,500 men: Hitler decreed that 12,300 men was the requisite number to justify retreat. Machorka-Muff is promoted to General, and lays the cornerstone of the «College of Military Memories» (shades of Franju's *Hôtel des Invalides*). He takes this occasion to establish that Hurlanger-Hiss in fact lost 14,700 men before retreating. The next day he marries his mistress, after her priest has assured her that, since she is Protestant, her seven previous marriages don't count. On their honeymoon, news arrives that the new Military Academy is under verbal fire from the opposition. However, Machorka-Muff and his old army friends have the majority in Parliament, and to allay any further concern, his aristocratic wife assures him that her family has never been successfully opposed.

Straub has made it clear that, of all his films, this was one of the most explicitly political in intention:

Machorka-Muff *is the story of a rape, the rape of a country on which an army has been imposed, a country which would have been happier without one.* (in Roud, 1971, p.29)

The reason I wanted to make a film about it at once was precisely my first strong political feelings, as I was still a student in Strasbourg, and which I still had, that was my first bout of political rage – exactly this story of the European defence community, i.e. the fact that Germany had re-armed – the story of a rape. That is to say, the only country in Europe which, after a certain Napoleon, the first gangster in the series, had the chance to be free. This chance was destroyed. I know for a fact that in Hamburg people threw stones at the first uniforms, i.e. people didn't want them, they had had enough of it. (Straub, 1970, p.17)

Straub's protest against re-armament was predictably ill-received by the right in Germany, while the leftist critics, agreeing with his sentiments, objected to the style of his presentation. They felt that Machorka-Muff had not been sufficiently characterised as a militarist; he didn't look sufficiently «evil». One presumes that the model these critics looked towards was that of Eisenstein, whose coarsely satiric delineation of the Tsar's sycophantic forces in *October* or *Strike* set the mainstream example of «political» film's typage of actors. Straub displays little sympathy for this essentially expressionistic tradition, preferring to create a visual environment that is «correct» in every possible detail: thus he refuses to conform to a convention that decrees that evil men look evil. No individual can personify the qualities inherent in our reading of the collective unit, the Military.

Straub, then, ignores the potential for a vituperative caricature of «the Military mind». His portrait of Machorka-Muff centres not so much upon interpretation of his personality, as upon an agglomeration of documentary detail, seizing on elements of Machorka-Muff's environment that tell us far more about the mentality of post-war Germany than a caricatured presentation of the man could have implied. Straub's documentary mode establishes the context of individual actions with devastating precision. There is a profusion of tray-bearing servants throughout the film: their movements are always measured, even mechanical, but never sycophantic. Impersonality is the keynote, and the servants have no direct contact with anyone, everything passing through the intermediary of the white-covered tray; they are objects, rather than humans, to be summoned at the snap of two fingers. The notion of servitude runs through the film in other respects too: Inn becomes Machorka-Muff's servant, pouring his tea, holding his coat; a workman places the cornerstone Machorka-Muff purports to be laying; and, as a long newspaper montage makes clear, the church is at pains to be the lackey of the militarists: «Jesus objected not to the soldier's profession, but the whores'», shouts a headline. It is up to the audience to pick up the irony here – Christ forgave adultery, but was crucified by a military governor, in fact.

These various «services» are never obsequiously performed, however: it is the cold impersonality of proceedings, the cool efficiency and glassy crispness, detached from any personalised context, that betrays the moral inadequacies of «the Military». Machorka-Muff's relationship with Inn is equally passionless; he initially has difficulty making contact with her, he thinks about phoning, but doesn't, and then when she phones him, the message is cryptic, enigmatic. The nearest they come to physical passion is Machorka-Muff's formal peck at the back of her hand. And Straub's handling of the final scene in which Inn assures her husband that no one has ever successfully opposed her family, again reveals their lack of any moral dimension whatsoever: Inn's statement is delivered with unannounced aplomb, upon which the screen goes black and the film is over. The very flatness, abruptness of the ending drains any emotional juice from the statement: we are left to consider the words themselves, in cold objectivity – no interpretive phrasing or reflection is allowed to modulate the hardness of the words themselves, with their barrenly aristocratic ethos.

The revelation and critique of Machorka-Muff's ideology is accomplished through the accumulation of documentary detail, and its subtle sharpening by Straub's precise use of both camera and soundtrack. Thus a snap of the fingers to summon a waiter is transformed into a moment symbolising the spiritual essence of an authoritarian world. Machorka-Muff's stepping down at the close of his dedication speech becomes not merely an end, but a moment of crystallisation: Straub's camera is low, looking up at Machorka-Muff; when he steps down, the frame is empty – just the whiteness of the sky remains: we are presented with a visual and emotional vacuum, a void that is underpinned by the incursion on the soundtrack of the wittily lugubrious band, grinding out its dirge. The laying of the cornerstone that follows is similarly visualised in its barest essentials: a single take, from a high-angled camera, contains within the frame the cornerstone, Machorka-Muff and a workman. The workman lays mortar along the bricks; he lifts the stone slab and places it on top of the mortar (the diligence of the workman is counterpointed against the rigid inactivity of Machorka-Muff); Machorka-Muff ritualistically taps the slab with a hammer, three times. The ceremony is complete, and we are told that inside the cornerstone is secreted a photograph of Hurlanger-Hiss and one of his epaulets. There are no fawning crowds, no impressive officials, or celebratory overtones. Straub's visualisation is minimalist and documentary, rather than dramatic. And this is precisely its virtue. Pushed in this direction through his experience with, and admiration for Bresson (he had been his assistant on *Un Condamné à mort s'est échappé* in 1956), Straub believes in the necessity of spareness, of the elimination of non-essentials, in order to penetrate to the core of a situation. The very emptiness of the cornerstone sequence testifies to its spiritual essence: the evacuation of humanity, the near obscenity of the mucilaginous mortar, the obsessively formalistic tapping of the slab, the fetishism inherent in the preservation through incarceration of the photo and epaulet, all these details form Straub's critique of the ideology of Machorka-Muff. It is the revelatory capacity of his documentarism that constitutes Straub's political commentary.

In *Machorka-Muff,* Straub's emphasis on «the necessity of spareness» is not so much a radical innovation as it is a modification of the classical strategy of «form creating content»; that is, the emptiness and impersonality of his frames testify to the moral vacuity of his characters, his style «proves» his theme. But his subsequent films raise more complex problems. An ascetic aesthetic has never been a touchstone of European art, but the cinema does contain exponents of the doctrine in both Dreyer and Bresson, both of whom have consistently worked in an intensely *reflective* manner that required, as Paul Schrader puts it, «sacrifice of the vicarious enjoyments that cinema seems uniquely able to provide, empathy for character, plot, and fast movement». (Schrader, 1972, p. 112) The purpose of this sacrifice is the expression of «the Transcendent on film», and Richard Roud has suggested that Straub's films be seen in the context of this endeavour. There is, however, a crucial difference between the austerity of Bresson and that of Straub. Bresson pares away the non-essentials in order to enable the viewer to *feel* his way to the heart of the film; his end is epiphanous, transcendental. Straub's austerity is *functional,* it forces the audience to *think.* [. . .] Straub rejects any attempt to anaesthetise the mind of the viewer; he refuses to make concessions to his audience's expectations. We are never allowed to identify with the characters that inhabit his films; our eyes are not glutted by sweeping camera movements or cluttered frames. We cannot enter into his worlds: but we may reflect upon them, and the «spareness» of his style functions as an invitation to reflection, to analysis.

Straub's later films, in particular, create spaces in which, deliberately, nothing happens — they are spaces in which the eye and mind are *invited* to interact.

Straub's rejection of conventional narrative forms has been explicit right from the opening titles of *Machorka-Muff*, which state that the film is «an abstract-visual dream, not a story». Although there *is* a story at the base of *Machorka-Muff*, Straub's presentation, as we have seen, is focused on a second, analytic level of diegesis. Both levels are apparent in the opening scenes, in which we are given no means by which to orient ourselves to the narrative. A shot of a telephone, a pan along the skyline of a city at night, a man sleeping, followed by the eerie pomposity of three bowing statues, which are then revealed as being in the form of Machorka-Muff (the epic unveiling of his ego — thus stating Straub's intention in the film). This is succeeded by a shot of

«*Machorka Muff*»

Machorka-Muff shaving before a mirror, while the commentary intones (it is Machorka-Muff's voice) «a typical capital-city dream». This line pinpoints the film's dialectical method: there is a perpetual disjunction between Machorka-Muff's perception of himself and our perception of him. In this instance, the dream *he* refers to is the one we have just witnessed; but the image we confront as we hear the line «a typical capital-city dream» is of him shaving — Straub's framing presents it almost as a commercial for an electric razor, such is its confident glossiness. Machorka-Muff is himself the dream, in Straub's terms, the illusion of moral rectitude that must be revealed in all its falsehood.

The dialectical relationship that exists between image and sound frequently establishes Straub's critical stance. There is, for instance, the early scene in the hotel lounge where Machorka-Muff chats with Heffling (a subordinate, who is not distinguished by a double-barrelled name, symbolically); Heffling leaves, and Straub in a comparative long-shot observes Machorka-Muff walk with him to the door. The setting (the harshest of deco design), the lighting, the characters' movements, all express a rigid, formal propriety that Straub brilliantly undercuts through Machorka-Muff's musing on the soundtrack: «Maybe I'll have an affair with his wife, you never know what Cupid may keep in store . . .» The contradiction between the surface appearance and the subterranean reality of Machorka-Muff's world is brilliantly, and economically, given precision, revealing the hollowness of his pretensions towards «Honour, Decency», and concomitant Romantic-bourgeois notions. The conflict between theory and actuality is apparent again when Straub presents a conventional image of the newly married couple on their honeymoon, a waiter serving them champagne, Straub then satirically undercuts the image with Inn's single comment: «I always feel like this as a bride.»

For audiences who are perhaps better prepared to accept the soundtrack as a purely illustrative addition to the visuals, Straub's interdependence of sound and image has met with considerable hostility, both on the part of the film industry itself, and of an audience unable to appreciate the rigour of his logic. Of all his work, the film that most clearly exemplifies his attitude toward the use of sound is *The Chronicle of Anna Magdalena Bach*, one of the most beautiful achievements in film history. It is built around the triple axes of music, image and commentary, music being the central component out of which the other two elements grow. Unusual, even unique, though this procedure may be, it is predicated on Straub's respect for the material elements of his discourse.

Bach's music is obviously the most authentic data we have on the man's mind and personality, and Straub presents this quite unadulterated. The other information the film offers, both visual and verbal, is of secondary authenticity, to the extent that it is dependent upon actors, upon manuscripts by hands other than Bach's, and upon destroyed buildings. Straub never attempts an illusionist film, we are never invited to consider it a literal reconstruction. Instead, where authenticity is impossible to achieve, he prefers to make the impossibility explicit, creating a subtle dialogue between the eighteenth and twentieth centuries. One point at which it erupts quite expressionistically is a scene in which Bach, playing the organ in the foreground, is set against the facade of a building in the rear. Since the eighteenth century, the original building has been destroyed, and instead of faking the scene, Straub deliberately emphasises the fact that the building is a back-projected image — not only is there agitation of the foreground, emphasising its separateness from the background, but the two are tilted at opposite angles on the frame, making the unreality absolutely explicit.

The image itself is beautiful; Straub's placement of a burning torch on the left side of the frame clinching the poise of the composition. The shot is a meditation about the distance between the eighteenth and twentieth centuries – the impossibility and undesirability of accurate reconstruction. Instead of attempting a complete illusion of reality, the artifice is deliberately underlined. The artifice is offset by the placement of the burning torch, which functions as a symbol of the continuing, eternal vitality of the music, even if the man and his environment are lost. The emphatic artifice serves both to highlight the unassailable beauty and integrity of the music itself, and to reinforce our awareness of the limitations of the documentary mode.

For what makes Straub an inherently political film-maker is not his choice of subject matter, but his approach to that subject matter, his respect for the integrity of his materials. The search for truth is at the root of all his films; this truth can only rise out of documentarism, a documentarism that reflects on the degree of its truth: this for Straub is the root of political thinking:

> *The revolution is like God's grace, it has to be made anew each day, it becomes new every day, a revolution is not made once and for all. And it's exactly like that in daily life. There is no division between politics and life, art and politics. I think one has no other choice, if one is making films that can stand on their own feet, they must become documentary, or in any case they must have documentary roots. Everything must be correct, and only from then on can one rise above, reach higher.* (1970, p. 20)

This explains the skeletal basis of the *Bach* film: each of its three axes is subjected to the same rigorous scrutiny and presentation. The spoken language portion (principally Anna Magdalena's monologue) derives chiefly from various eighteenth-century texts – Bach's letters, a necrology written by one of his sons. Straub and his wife, Danièle Huillet, worked this material into the monologue form, preserving the original form of the language. What we have is a kind of documentary fiction: its presentation is consonant with this, it being read in a non-interpretative monotone; no emotional «bending» of the material is allowed. The musical performances that flow through the entire film are, quite literally, documentary, since Straub insisted on shooting with synchronous sound. The visuals too are documentary in the purest sense: a simple recording of the performances, with functional distances and angles: very few close-ups, high-angles used where necessary – as in observing Bach playing the organ, when we need to see both the movement of his hands on the keys, and feet on the pedals. Elsewhere, the visuals consist of gently panning shots across the original sheet music, and other manuscripts.

The documentary foundation of the film demanded, predictably, a good deal of historical research. Like Rossellini's *The Rise to Power of Louis XIV*, *Anna Magdalena Bach* sets out to present historically verifiable facts on the screen in

«Anna Magdalena Bach»

the most coldly objective manner possible; they cannot be tampered with. What Paul Schrader has said of Rossellini's film, is as true of Straub's:

> *Because Rossellini makes no attempt to plunge the viewer into the drama of the past, making the past relevant to his immediate feelings . . . the viewer has a sense of detachment rather than involvement, of awareness rather than empathy.* (Schrader, 1970, vol. 6, no. 3, p.4)

In the Rossellini film, this detachment is partly due to the presence of a voice-over narrator, whose omniscient, contemporary presence contrasts with Straub's use of the voice of Anna Magdalena, who remains ensnared in the eighteenth century: her deadpan delivery, however, establishes a distance that works in a manner close to that of Rossellini, though it retains traces of a (suppressed because understated) personal intensity not present in *The Rise to Power of Louis XIV.* Where it was possible for Straub to be authentic, he went to great pains to achieve it. In 1958 (ten years before he finally raised financing for the film), he went to East Germany, to visit the various towns Bach had been associated with; Straub says he did this *not only because of the towns, which in the end are not shown in the film at all. It was there I understood that one couldn't make the film in the original surroundings at all, because these have been altered in the nineteenth century. The Thomas school where Bach lived for thirty years was torn down around 1900. The Thomas church in Leipzig was altered by an organ in a horrible neo-gothic style . . .* (1970, p. 15)

Instead of trying to shoot on non-existent locations, Straub decided to limit his frame to interiors and the musicians themselves. The slow process of reconstructing what could be done began: even the musicians' spectacles are correct:

We got the formula for the glasses for each of the musicians, and we made corresponding spectacles for those who couldn't play without them . . . There are some original instruments among the ones we used, the oboes are all original; there are also copies, the violins, for instance, they used to play standing, which is not done any more, and the violinists played without the chin-support . . . Also, when we had a white transparent window in a church, it was because during the Renaissance and most of all during the early Baroque, most of the Gothic stained glass windows were dismantled and replaced by white glass. (ibid.)

A concomitant to this painstaking sense of detail was the exposure of certain myths concerning our conventional image of what the period looked like. For instance the characters wear no make-up:

There is a contradiction between wigs and faces that have no make-up. And I didn't want to do what they told me, what they usually do in films. They accepted that, and the wigs have tulle as foundation, and it is visible underneath, it can be concealed with make-up, but I wanted to make it so that the wig is recognised as such. At that time it was like a hat or a sign of affluence, they just put it on their heads, and didn't want to make it look like real hair, as is customary in films. (ibid.)

Just as the instruments are replicas of the original forms, so Leonhardt, the musician who plays the role of Bach, plays as Bach did — with his thumb, an unorthodox method; similarly, Straub refuses to conform to notions of the baroque cluttering the furniture — asceticism is the mode, and it is accurate.

All this serves, of course, to explain Straub's insistence on the necessity for direct sound: overdubbing or post-synchronisation would amount to falsification, cheating. This insistence is not of significance for the audience, nor even for critical evaluation of the film as an aesthetic object (it is, after all, difficult to decipher such details from a film soundtrack in a movie theatre); rather it is indicative of Straub's concern for honesty at the level of his *production* procedure. If the musicians are to be seen playing music, then the music heard must be «correct» to the extent of synchronous recording. This desire for truth in his films has a further conceptual rationale: it involves the recognition of the fact that any attempt to portray the *personality* of the man, Johann Sebastian Bach, would be futile. What we evidently see is a young musician *playing* Bach — a fact which Straub does not wish to obscure — and it is a major reason in his decision to use non-professional actors. For actors are trained to stop being themselves, to try to slip into a fictional figure. Any such procedure would be dishonest, in Straub's eyes, so all Leonhardt does is play music — no *acting* is demanded of him, just as no *interpretation* of her script is required by the actress who plays Anna — she just intones it in a monotone; the fact that she finally achieves a rare incantatory beauty is a happy result of Straub's initial procedural rigour. Straub makes no attempt to establish either Bach or Anna as «real eighteenth-century people», for the ephemeral personal details that provide the core of Ken Russell's self-indulgent «musical biographies» have no place in Straub's aesthetic. Such details are never visualised, and are only mentioned when crucial: such as those points where the death of their first two children is calmly, matter-of-factly announced, as we watch Anna playing a delicate piece: «Death robbed us of our first-born and second-born.» The flatness of the delivery lends it great pathos, but the music's ability to transcend such ephemeral (in the context of the present) detail is again underlined. A similarly symbolic moment occurs when Bach is arrested while conducting his choir: another conductor steps in as Bach is marched off, and the music continues unfalteringly, as if impervious to mortal dramas.

Always it is the music rather than the personality that is the central focus, and this recognition is evident as much in what *is* in the film, as in what is left out. Usually Straub presents us with the whole group of musicians playing, refusing to single out any individual. Bach is often to be found hidden in the depth of the frame, or placed near its edge; in this way Straub minimises the *dramatic* possibilities, preferring to visualise Bach's elimination of his self in favour of his music. When we do get a close-up of Bach, playing a clavier piece near the end of the film, it is for functional reasons: our attention is directed to his eyes, which are soon to fail. In general, Straub makes us listen to the music, he refuses to divert us visually, just as he refuses to hypothesise on the nature of Bach's feelings at any point. By choosing to *play* the music, he makes the viewer draw his own imaginative conclusions on the feelings. Straub's artistry is inclusive of his audience, he compels us to participate in the creation of the film's «meaning»; we cannot remain passive. (Of course, if the viewer is there merely to be entertained, s/he is likely to become bored; indeed few people are prepared to *think* their way through films, and this in part accounts for Straub's relatively small audience.)

Having achieved a certain documentary truth and accuracy, Straub transcends this level to, in his own words, «rise above documentary to aim at something higher». Now it is exceedingly difficult to precisely locate the source of the film's beauty, but it is my experience that the film creates a quite extraordinary serenity that is beyond the limits of «mere documentarism». This results from the complex interaction of the musical, visual and verbal elements, which Straub orchestrates with stunning sensitivity. One aspect of this is the close and moving identity that exists between the film's form and its subject.

The rigorous clarity of the music finds its counterpart (counterpoint) in the ascetic simplicity of Straub's visual presentation. There are almost no close-ups, pans, dissolves, or other camera tricks. (Varying lengths of pause on the verbal track are used to indicate the passing of time, instead of dissolves.) The organisation of the compositions, their relation to each other, is a formal reiteration of the music's own structure. Straub's use of diagonal perspectives isn't merely a functonal one (functional in that it facilitates inclusiveness, creates a sense of depth, of perspective, and so on); these diagonals also have a formal structural values. Straub tends to rhythmically alternate the direction of these diagonals (left to right, right to left), creating an equivalent for the contrapuntal mode of Bach's music. Rather than merely illustrating Bach's music in some manner, Straub has found a structural equivalent for it; as Richard Roud writes:

> *Throughout the film he plays with binary symmetry, left-right polarity, and the changing direction of his diagonals both in the camera set-ups and in the camera movements . . . There is even an extraordinary pair of shots, one in the first third of the film, and another symmetrically in the last third, which are almost mirror-images one to the other; as in a mirror-fugue, a popular musical device of Bach's day where every note is reversed, the angle and placing of the actors is completely reversed.* (Roud, op. cit., pp. 78–9)

The strongly formal sense of the film is in many ways simply a reflection of the formal, even mathematical, basis of much Baroque music — after all, rhythm is inherently a mathematical concern, a measuring process, and Straub has a clear grasp of this in both the small and large units of the film. The two shots of the sea, and the one of the sky, function in this rhythmic sense also, being almost equidistantly placed. The discussion of rhythm and measure is difficult, however, because it can only be *felt* to be relevant — its effect is emotionally apprehended, and analysis of its cause can never *prove* the effect. Nevertheless, the sea-shots are not dependent upon their rhythmic placement for their importance, they have another relevance — their pictorial beauty and appropriateness. They function as breathing spaces on the film, a moment of release from enclosure, a moment, quite literally, of transcendence of the characteristically tightly framed interiors. And their composition is equally literally transcendent; beside being a mode of punctuation, both the sea and sky shots *lift* the eyes upwards. Both images are composed with a dark area on the lower half of the frame (either pebbles or trees), and the eyes move naturally to the lighter area, which is upwards, paralleling the uplifting music; but it is not distractive – the still, ethereal image allows one to concentrate upon the complexity of the music; as in the rest of the film, Straub's visuals highlight the brilliant vitality of Bach's music.

It is significant that Bach only speaks at rare moments in the course of the film; Anna is the biographer, events are seen from her external viewpoint. We remain outside Bach in the interests of objectivity; when he *does* speak, it is in connection with poverty, begging for cash; we hear him pleading the necessity for the advancement of musical art, the need for the encouragement of musical innovations. It is important that we hear this from Bach, rather than Anna. Straub is in many ways close to the traditional definition of the Japanese artist: «One who makes every attempt to obscure his personal, idiosyncratic tendencies in order to create a more impersonal universal expression.» (Schrader, 1970, vol. 6, no. 1, p.2) Straub's overt presence is certainly rare in his films, and I think we are invited to take those moments when Bach *does* speak in the film as being special moments: Bach's plea for advancement and innovation is read as Straub's plea for advancement and innovation in film. It is at these points that we realise just how closely committed Straub is to everything that Bach represents. And it is his breaking of the mould of objectivity (Anna's monotone) that constitutes his admission of this identity. Straub's ten-year struggle to make the film, to raise the finances for it, lends authority to the unexpected personal eruptions of Bach himself into the reflective texture of *The Chronicle of Anna Magdalena Bach*. Straub has quite openly admitted his sense of parallel between himself and Bach:

> *... this film interested me, because Bach was precisely someone who reacted against his own inertia, although he was deeply rooted in his times, and was oppressed.* (1970, p.17)

All of Straub's work is, in one sense or another, a reaction against his own inertia. *Machorka-Muff* was an attempt at a meaningful response to a politically repressive occurrence, and both *Not Reconciled* (1964–5) and *Othon* are attempts to come to terms with, and comprehend, history. Straub's oblique approach to the problem of Germany's Nazi past resulted in *Not Reconciled,* which was adapted from Heinrich Böll's novel, *Billiards at Half-Past Nine.* However, the source of the film is not a particularly helpful place to commence a critical analysis (*pace* Richard Roud) since the best it can do is attempt to unravel a singularly difficult cinematic experience. Straub, indeed, would prefer us to forget the novelistic source:

> *I believe one can't make a film of any book – because one films something about a book or with a book, but never of a book – one films always from one's own experience. A film lives and exists only when it is based on the experiences of the so-called director.* (ibid., p.19)

«Not Reconciled»

Straub takes as his starting point the principle that film is «a perceptual present» – that there is, in our experience of watching a film, no past tense. He then transfers this idea to the narrative organisation, eliding all the connectives that were present in Böll's novel, thereby formally underlining the historical principle that present and past are indivisible. Again we note Straub's proximity to Marxist theory: «Not only the result, but the road to it also, is a part of the truth», Marx noted, and Straub's maieutic endeavour in *Not Reconciled,* to objectify the latent tendencies of the German nation, is predicated on this principle. The process of our struggle to come to terms with the film runs parallel with the protagonist Robert Fähmel's attempt to come to terms with his past.

As he had earlier done with *Machorka-Muff,* Straub attacked his subject from an oblique angle:

The fact which interested me was to make a film about Nazism without mentioning the word Hitler or concentration camps and such things that a middle-class family did not suspect or want to suspect. (ibid.)

In its individual elements, the film is congruent with the characteristic constituents of Straub's style: the documentary mode, the flat monotony of the actors' dialogue, an ascetic camera style. The elision of Böll's transitional statements reinforces the generalised image of the nation, rather than the intimacies of family relations. Everything in the film pushes beyond the boundaries of the personal, to the national. One might even say that impersonality is a central motif; like Machorka-Muff's solitariness (eating alone, walking alone) the characters in *Not Reconciled* are alone, set in a hostilely impersonal environment. One shot that clinches this mood of pessimism is a 360° panning shot around a suburban desert, which culminates on a young man standing at a door; a child informs him that the person he seeks has never been there. Straub consistently uses empty spaces — often to create a sense that it is a space that has been vacated by those that don't «fit in» — like Robert's mother who has been committed to an insane asylum because she called the Kaiser «a fool». The barren nature of the environment is perhaps due, Straub seems to suggest, to the fact that the eliminative principles of Nazism have rendered it spiritually sterile.

Like *Othon*, so too *The Bridegroom, The Comedienne and the Pimp* (1968), a short film that Straub completed shortly after *The Chronicle of Anna Magdalena Bach*, may be considered as a reflection on film expression. Indeed all of his films, largely as a result of his minimalist visual style, can be seen as essentially self-reflexive. Straub has consistently tested and re-evaluated the basic elements of the cinematic experience. In *The Chronicle of Anna Magdalena Bach*, for instance, montage is entirely absent, each sequence is autonomous, and allows the music to swell and take on a life of its own. The static camera, like that of Lumière (or D. W. Griffith, whom Straub has particularly made references to), invites us to watch for slight movements (leaves, musicians' hands, wigs) within the frame, and view them as if they had never been seen before on a screen. In *Othon*, the long scene by the fountain, with Othon and Plautine dressed in red and white, with the blanket of green grass and water as their backdrop, is both a meditation on the use of colour and, through the insistent noise of the fountain throughout the scene, a gesture of homage to Bresson's *Les Dames du Bois de Boulogne*. In the films before *The Bridegroom*, however, reflections upon problems of cinematic expression were subsumed in the larger subject of each; in this 23-minute film, Straub uses his simple plot as a central core around which he can explore the expressive possibilities of cinema. The film grew, Straub tells us, out of two things:

> *It was born out of the impossible May revolution in Paris . . . it is based on a news-item (there is nothing more political than a news-item) about the romance between an ex-prostitute and a negro, seen in relation to a text extracted from a play by Ferdinand Bruckner.* (Roud, op. cit., p.87)

The narrative may be summarised thus: a middle-class girl is put to work on

«The Bridegroom, the Comedienne, and the Pimp»

the streets by her boyfriend pimp. She meets a negro, falls in love. After fleeing from the wrath of the pimp, they are married. They arrive home to find the pimp awaiting them. She shoots the pimp, and their love triumphs. One's first viewing of the film may not, however, seem to match up to this description, since Straub has meticulously broken the film down into stylistically autonomous fragments. There are twelve shots in the film, and they form seven units which have, at first sight, little to do with each other.

The first unit comprises the titles, which appear over graffiti, among which we discern the statement, «Stupid old Germany, I hate it over here, I hope I can go soon, Patricia». The second consists of a long tracking shot (the first half of which is silent, the second accompanied by Bach's «Ascension Oratorio»), which runs interminably down the prostitutes' row of Munich. The third consists of an entire three-act stage-play, which lasts ten minutes, shot in a single take.* The fourth consists of a thriller-style chase. The fifth is a wedding ceremony. The sixth is a mystical slow pan that commences on an empty field, until magically a car is conjured out of nothing, and the camera seizes on it. The seventh segment is the shooting sequence, preceded by verses

---

*In fact the three acts are divided by short lengths of black spacing.

from St. John of the Cross. Only this final segment, the transcendental moment of the film, is in a style that we would recognise as pure Straub. The preceding six are, rather, a meditation upon the other stylistic possibilities of the cinema and in their sequential organisation they constitute the history of that cinema; and the mood of the film's development, both in terms of its plot, and its aesthetic meditation, is crystallised by the tonal difference between the first and last images. The darkness and gloom of the Landsbergerstrasse is transformed into the shimmering light of the sky and trees of the final shot.

In what sense do I mean *The Bridegroom* . . . constitutes the history of the cinema? The scene on the Landsbergerstrasse, like the image of the graffiti, is absolutely non-interpretative – the camera simply *records* reality, like Lumière did. (The very darkness of the shot implies a «fallen» Lumière, though.) Then, through variations of the car's pace of movement, and the unexpected movement of another car on the street, the camera discovers its power to manipulate our emotions, expectations. The introduction of the Bach on the soundtrack further transforms our response – it contradicts the visual reality before us. A dialectic of sound and image is established. Then the stage-play commences; rather than a production of Bruckner, it is a critique of Bruckner, Straub having concentrated the original text into its essential elements. These elements are those of bourgeois drama; what Straub leaves us with is the empty shell of melodrama, with its intrigues and sexual games; the facade of psychological observation is stripped away; the deliberateness of cues is emphatically exposed – as when at a point of revelation, someone enters to thwart that revelation; the actors mechanically adopt «meaningful» postures, exposing the manipulative mode that we know Straub decries. The actors come and go through the two doors of the set like so many robots – the empty ritual of bourgeois drama is mercilessly exposed – and intelligently so. Straub's attack is not negative, for one senses that in clearing out these relics of theatrical practice, he is actively ushering in a new style. The long take that envelops the play is both a reference to the earliest films, those static «filmed plays» that comprised the early history of film (and the early years of «talkies»), and a critical observation of that style. This critical attitude is enforced partly by Straub's characteristic diagonal camera angle which, in its very difference from the flat-on angles of the early Edison and Méliès films, emphasises Straub's (and our) critical stance. One of the lines from Bruckner's play that Straub retains is from Goethe: «Even in science, nothing is known, everything is to be done.» And the same, of course, applies to cinema.

The fourth segment of the film comprises five shots: the negro, James, leaves Lilith's apartment; he is followed by the pimp when he drives away; they chase across a bridge; by a gorge; up a scrubby hill. The sequence seems to bear no relation to what has preceded it – the stage-play. But the end of the stage-play consisted of Frede's decision to put his girlfriend to work on the streets. And Frede is played by the same person who plays the pimp (Rainer

Werner Fassbinder, another figure of the German theatrical and cinematic avant-garde): the continuity of person forces us to realise the continuity of narrative, elliptical though it may be. The chase sequence constitutes Straub's examination of the thriller genre. His sense of angles and lighting is correct: for instance, when James leaves the apartment, and comes to his car, Straub's camera is by the pimp's car — thus setting protagonist and assailant in conflict in the frame; and again, when the cars chase across the narrow bridge, Straub's camera sits at the end of the bridge, with the car and its headlights rushing dramatically at the lens. But Straub's critique of the mode is enforced by the way he evacuates each image of all the tension it has accrued, by holding the shot way past the theoretical cutting point. In the first instance, where an «action» director would cut when the cars moved off, Straub simply holds the shot until all movement has disappeared. In the second, Straub actually undercuts the mode during the chase: as the first car comes off the end of the bridge, Straub pans to follow its dramatic course, but instead of then panning back to pick up the arrival of the second car with all the dramatic tensions implicit in such a conventional procedure, he simply holds on the now motionless first car, until the second one finally arrives in the frame of its own accord. In other words, throughout this sequence of images, Straub, while appearing to conform to the mode of the thriller, actually evacuates the impact from each shot, thereby exposing the overtly manipulative strategies demanded by this style of film-making.

After the thriller, or Hollywood, came the resurgence of documentary, and particularly *cinéma-vérité*. And this is the mode of the fifth sequence: a long single take of the wedding ceremony between James and Lilith. And, as the *cinéma-vérité* movement discovered for itself, the mode fails to penetrate to any essential truths: this at least is what Straub suggests by his decision to depict the wedding ceremony with such literal objectivity. It is both boring and theatrical — linking it in fact to the earlier stage-play sequence. Unlike Straub's documentarism, this one doesn't bear the seeds of its own transcendence. And then comes the near-mystical sixth segment: a long-shot of a field, a few buildings in the far distance, and trees. After a few moments, almost miraculously there appears a vehicle, right out of the centre of the image — the camera pans slowly to hold it central in the frame, until finally the car almost fills the screen. This astonishing shot, in its context within this intensely metaphorical film, quite simply represents the rebirth of cinema, movement coming out of stasis.

And so to the final, seventh segment: James and Lilith address each other in the language of St. John of the Cross. James has come to «Buy the bride free who has served under a hard yoke.» Thematically this sums up the development of the narrative — the freeing of a prostitute, and it foreshadows the shooting of the pimp, lending humanist authority to the killing, after which their love is free and fulfilled, and the camera can, to the strains of

Bach's «Ascension Oratorio», track into the ecstatic, shimmering final image of sky and trees. But Lilith is not the only prostitute to be freed. The other is art, specifically film art, which, in the course of these 23 minutes, has evolved through its principal historical stages, until reaching its liberation in the materialist presentation that is Straub's own. The killing of the pimp is, metaphorically, the killing of Germany's decadent cultural heritage — the specifically German implication being raised in the graffiti that opened the film: «Stupid old Germany, I hate it over here, I hope I can go soon . . .» Straub has laid «stupid old Germany» to rest, the cinema has been liberated from its stifling conventions, and the film's movement from the sordid opening to the celebratory close cements the significance of this new beginning. Certainly, *The Bridegroom, The Comedienne and the Pimp* is one of Straub's most difficult films, the near total elimination of the narrative proving a major obstacle for many viewers. But in the context of the post-New Wave film, its importance is unmistakable: the self-reflexive linguistic questioning places Straub in the central European tradition of Brecht and Godard. In the rigorously logical development of his work from the materialist documentarism of *Machorka-Muff* to the exquisitely intelligent probing of *The Bridegroom . . .*, Straub's political integrity remains absolutely unmarked: he refuses to pre-package a message, he demands that we participate in the production of meaning, we do not consume his films, we participate in their creation of sense. In much major contemporary art, as Peter Wollen notes:

The text then becomes the location of thought, rather than the mind. The text is the factory where thought is at work, rather then the transport system which conveys the finished product. (Wollen, 1972, p. 164)

This precisely encapsulates the nature of Straub's cinematic texts, as it does that of Godard's. If we value Godard, or Makavejev, or Eisenstein, or Vertov, then it is necessary now to add the name of Jean-Marie Straub to that hierarchy of explorers of cinematic potential.

This article originally appeared in *Jump Cut,* No. 4, 1974, and is republished here by kind permission with only minor alterations. The contribution of Danièle Huillet to the films by her and Straub is duly acknowledged by the editors of *Jump Cut* and of this anthology.

«*History Lessons*»:
Brecht and Straub/Huillet

What Brechtian dramaturgy postulates is that today at least the responsibility of a dramatic art is not so much to express reality as to signify it. Hence there must be a certain distance between signified and signifier: revolutionary art must admit a certain arbitrary nature of signs, it must acknowledge a certain «formalism» . . . Roland Barthes (1972, pp.74–5).

Between 1941 and 1947, Brecht resided in the United States. During his time in what he called «cette morgue de l'easy-going», Brecht came to several conclusions about the cinema, conclusions not only about Hollywood, but about the very «nature» of film itself.

Above all I believe that the effect of an actor's performance on the spectator is not independent of the spectator's effect upon the actor. In the theatre, the public regulates the representation. The cinema in this respect has enormous weaknesses which seem theoretically insurmountable . . . The rigid fixation of the perspective: we see nothing except what the single camera eye has registered . . . Due to the fact of mechanical reproduction, everything tends to present itself as a finished result, constraining, unchangeable. We return to the fundamental reproach: the public has no opportunity to modify the actor's performance, he does not find himself confronting a production, *but the* result *of that production, which was produced in his absence.*
(Entry of 27 March 1942, in Brecht's *Arbeitsjournal*, published in French in *Cahiers du Cinéma* nos. 254-5, 1974)

[. . .]

History Lessons is based on parts of Brecht's «fragment-novel», *The Business Deals of Mr Julius Ceasar*. While Brecht was in Santa Monica, William Dieterle had had plans to make a film from this work, perhaps on the basis of the anecdotal elements which Straub/Huillet eliminated from their treatment. Even within the economic-historical discourses that remain in Straub/Huillet's text, there is sufficient material (wars, homosexuals, slaves) to gladden the heart of any producer. All they had to do was hand Brecht's final treatment over to their own scriptwriters! In fact, production capital was never raised, and Brecht was spared the anger of witnessing another mutilation of his work. But it is a pity he never lived to see *History Lessons*: it would be interesting to know whether he would reconsider his naming of the «fundamental reproach».

For the first and most immediate issue that *History Lessons* engages with is that, exactly, of production: the extent to which the audience must co-produce, rather than consume a given meaning. Following the title and the credits, the first four shots are tersely enigmatic: first, a series of three maps of the Roman Empire which successively diminish the Empire's territory through their total 8 seconds duration (a wittily speedy fall); and then, a statue of Caesar, one which is a replica, installed by Mussolini, of a statue erected some years after Caesar's death to celebrate (establish?) his mythological stature. The fifth shot is even more enigmatic. And to some viewers it contains less «facts», «information» than its predecessors: it is merely a man driving a car through a city: it is boring, nothing happens — so you leave the cinema. Or you begin to *create* connections, possible meanings, test them against each other, alongside each other.

What happens in this car-driving sequence (and the two later in the film) is indeed very little, if our definition of an *event* in film is one whose elements are strictly codified: if cinema exists, in other words, for the sake of the signified, rather than the signifier. For there appears to be little signification in this almost nine-minute shot — there is no (single) meaning. But there is a lot of sense, as opposed to signification, a lot of space to ruminate upon the process and procedures of meaning, upon history, time, aesthetics, upon the place and ideology of the spectator. And slowly the density of the shot opens out for us.

How may we see/hear this first drive? Firstly, we might note that this [fifth] shot is the third «History Lesson» the film offers us. First, a geographical — or, more accurately, territorial — history through the maps. Second, the statue: monumental history, Caesar the heroic individual, mythic man. Thirdly, the drive through the streets: it might be objected, following Brecht, that «the simple reproduction of reality says nothing at all about that reality». But this shot has been «literarised», captioned in such a way as to lead us into an active interrogation of its function: its caption is the film's title, *History Lessons* — the only words we have encountered (aside from the credits). So the first question we ask may be: «what has this to do with *History Lessons?*» And of course there's no one answer — simply a series of propositions.

An initial observation might be that the drive is «like history» — the problem is to seize moments for analysis, draw knowledge out of chaos: systematise flux, immobilise flow, in order to attempt to comprehend it. An image of history as a maze, a labyrinth into which we enter in our search for a centre, a security of knowledge. [. . .] More specifically, if this is a history lesson, what does it tell us? Firstly, that this history lesson is not interested in the usual sites of «historic interest». The version of history inaugurated in the [fourth] shot through the statue of Caesar is ignored on the drive: no sight-seeing here, no procession of monuments to a glorious past: the very tendency of Brecht's text, its demythologisation of Caesar, is here prefigured. Nor do we reach a museum — no institutional history is offered. What site of historic interest remains? Should we see these ranks of cars as the new monuments of our times — the automobile industry is a major nexus of capitalism, after all. Perhaps, but, as with the statue of Caesar, the crucial necessity for history is to penetrate the facade of monumentalisation, to uncover the processes of production that the ranks of cars block. (Such an endeavour is the Dziga Vertov group's *British Sounds*).

Should we then, after all, say that Brecht's reservations about «the simple reproduction of reality» apply here, that no useful history can be derived from the drive? Not necessarily: for the drive is through the streets of Rome, which brings several things to mind. This is modern Rome, not Caesar's Rome: but it is nevertheless Caesar's legacy to us, this capitalism whose traces cover the screen through the duration of the drive (traces that are virtually absent from the remainder of the film's images). So immediately the sense of *distance* between Caesar's time and our own, and the *connection* between them, are invoked. We may say that one of the functions of the driving sequences is to make space for a theorisation on the part of the viewer, of what may be involved in the notion of history in this film, of what may be involved in his confrontation with history through film. At this point it is helpful to recall some of Walter Benjamin's words in «Theses on the Philosophy of History»:

History is the subject of a structure whose site is not homogeneous empty time, but time filled by the presence of the now [Jetztzeit]. (Benjamin, 1970, p.261)

That is to say, this History Lesson is one whose *raison d'être* is exactly our contemporary situation — a period in which the heroisation of Caesar has been reinstituted by Mussolini, in which the mythologisation of individual «great men» is rampant (Churchill, Kennedy, etc.), in which the automobile has become the central «symbol of our times»:

To articulate the past historically does not mean to recognise it «the way it really was» (Ranke). It means to seize hold of a memory as it flashes up at a moment of danger. Historical materialism wishes to retain that image of the past which unexpectedly appears to man singled out by history at a moment of danger. The danger affects both the content of the tradition and its receivers. The same threat hangs over both: that of becoming a tool of the ruling classes. In every era the attempt must be made anew to wrest tradition away from a conformism that is about to overpower it. (ibid.)

So the thrust of *History Lessons* will be to replace Caesar in a context that is useful for us today—an economic and social history that «wrests tradition away from conformism». Brecht's text blasts open the myth of the Roman Empire as a homogeneous unit with clearly defined aims, he reveals it to be riddled with contradictions, conflicts of interest (the slave issue, for example). It makes clear that a crucial issue is not Caesar himself, but where his ideas and power came from (the battles, struggles, persecutions of the Gracchi family). Gradually it becomes clear that Caesar is the prototype of the modern capitalist, and the drive sequences take on a further resonance: the car factories we never see are the modern version of what the Banker describes near the end of the film:

And the mountain valleys resound today with the peaceful hammering in the metal pits and with the merry call of the slaves.

These pits and these slaves are what history books prefer to ignore, and Brecht's principal achievement is exactly the overturning of «tradition». To use Benjamin's phrase, Brecht «brushes history against the grain», and we may say the same of Straub/Huillet, in respect of their choice of texts to film. Their recent films have all been based upon works relatively unappropriated by the culture-mongers: *Othon* is a Corneille play that had, apparently, not been performed since 1707; both the Brecht text for *History Lessons* and Schoenberg's *Moses and Aaron* are unfinished works which the Western cultural pantheon prefers to ignore, since they lack the appropriate unity, closure, completion. Here again the connection to Benjamin is clear:

As flowers turn toward the sun, by dint of a secret heliotropism, the past strives to turn toward that sun which is rising in the sky of history. A historical materialist must be aware of this most inconspicuous of all transformations.

[. . .] in all of their films, Straub/Huillet have been close to Benjamin's formulation of the task of the historical materialist:

Historicism gives the «eternal» image of the past; historical materialism supplies a unique experience with the past. (Benjamin, 1970, op.cit.)

This formulation certainly contributes towards an explanation of their attitude to history in *History Lessons,* and it is one that is clarified by contrast to Rossellini's «historical» films, whether *The Rise to Power of Louis XIV* or *Socrates* or any of his recent films. For Rossellini indeed attempts to reconstitute the past «the way it really was», attempts to find «the eternal image of the past». Straub/Huillet resist any desire to situate us within the world of the past. If we view the car drive as a journey, a search for «history», then the first sequence with the Banker clarifies immediately their Brechtian notion of how that history must be presented: the lack of eye-contact between the young man and the banker, their difference in dress (contemporary and «historical»), the mode of the Banker's verbal delivery, the lack of any historical setting (all we see are the brown, dusty ground, and some lilac bushes), all of these deny us entry into Caesar's world. Whereas the opening shots of *The Rise to Power of Louis XIV* explicitly convey the audience from the riverbank outside the court *into* the court environment, within which we then remain for the duration of the film as *witnesses* to «how it really was» — we are offered the «truth», the eternal image of how Louis cemented his power. In *History Lessons,* on the other hand, we never see Caesar, he remains a hypothetical presence, talked about, placed, constructed not in terms of personality, but of power relations. The interview with the peasant is wittily symptomatic in this respect:

Q: *Did you see him [Caesar] from near?*
A: *500 steps one time, 1000 steps the other time; once at a parade in Lucus, which meant 4 more hours exercise; the other time at the embarking for Britain.*
Q: *He was much loved?*
A: *He passed as smart.*
Q: *But the simple soldier had confidence in him?*
A: *The food was not bad. He saw to that, so they said.*

The distance between the questions and the answers (clearly not those expected or wanted by the interviewer) is crucial to Brecht's intention as to Straub/Huillet's: the demystification of the cult of the leader (the theme also of *Moses and Aaron,* Straub/Huillet's next subject).

The dialectical exchange between the young man and the peasant is typical of Brecht's textual organisation: see, for instance, the twin accounts of Caesar's encounter with the pirates. First the young man gives the «official» version, the one that represents Caesar as heroic, a «man of his word», as bowing to no man, etc. The way in which the young man is dressed, in white shirt and dark suit marks him as eminently a child of the theological establishment, for whom «the Book is the Word» — and Straub/Huillet continue this idea by making the young man's delivery of the «official» history appropriate to a catechism. The banker's version, on the other hand, resituates the myth in a specific economic/historical context, resurrects «inconveniences» for the heroic/idealist discourse of official history — inconveniences such as slave-trade, smuggling, extortion, self-serving barbarism, and so forth. As Walter Benjamin put it: «There is no document of civilisation which is not at the same time a document of barbarism.»

Another aspect of the car sequences that invites consideration has to do with the very nature of cinematic representation. The long unbroken takes exist here in dialectical opposition to the segmented construction of the scenes with the banker and the peasant. And where the latter mark an investigation of the operations of editing, these driving passages may be described as a meditation upon the process of representation, its compositional implications. First we note the series of frames that are on the screen: at the most obvious level, there is the frame delimited by the edge of the screen, that contains the interior of the car. Then there is the windscreen of the car, which is our «window upon the world», through which we gaze upon «reality». There is also a less conventional «window on the world» — in the roof of the car, a sliding roof which opens another frame, through which pass more oblique perspectives on the «real-world». The fourth frame is that contained in the driver's rear-view mirror, and in it we see his eyes and nose — through this mirror we find our link to the narrator (otherwise faceless, as befits his minimal visual presence in the film). Through this mirror we are, however, implicitly thrown back to ourselves, it enforces awareness of our position as specular subjects — the nature of our relationship to the images on the screen is raised once more. And the appositeness of Godard's Brechtian maxim that cinema is «not the reflection of reality, but the reality of the reflection» is also stressed, through the double reflections that occur within this series of frames: the windscreen bears the reflection of the driver's hands — thus becoming screen rather than window, and the glass of the speedometer dial reflects the sky passing overhead, via the hole in the roof. These series of frames within frames are important not only in so far as they underline the flatness of the screen (in direct opposition to the Bazinian elevation of the «long take» and «depth of focus» as the devices essential to a transparent capturing of an ineffable reality), but also relate to the notion of a distanciated history which is central to both Brecht and Straub/Huillet.

In this respect it is perhaps useful to think about how we see the world outside the car: fundamentally, it is perceived as *other*. People stream past, each with their separate histories; sounds, equally, pass in and out of our frame of vision and hearing. The problem is to decipher these alien moments, to make them intelligible: they offer a potential but unrealised history. The car passes through the streets, but we are never (as we would be in a Rossellini film) *in* the streets. Our point-of-view is one that has no tactile contact with the world of the streets — it is, in a sense, impenetrable, the interior of the car acts as an imprisoning capsule; there is a chasm we cannot cross — the unity of signifier/signified is denied us, as we are constantly aware of the materiality of the film-text, the means of articulation. No transparency here, as is emphasised in another manner by the lack of alteration of the camera's aperture as the car passes from open squares into narrow streets. This alternation of enclosed and open spaces may be read in terms of confinement and liberation, but in any event the shifts from very dark images to very bright ones emphasise the celluloid materiality — celluloid, unlike our eyes, does not adjust itself to register «perfect» images.

It is even possible to approach the drives in terms of narrative potential. Certainly there are moments of drama that could bear a symbolic weight: the red truck, for instance, or the blue truck marked with white lettering «Epiphani», the coincidental reference to Joyce being delightfully suggestive. In an interview, Straub mentioned as a reason for his consistent use of live synchronous sound recording, his desire

> ... to have surprises and to discover a reality. To experiment with combinations that are a great deal richer than those one might be able to find oneself, with one's petty intentions. It means giving myself the possibility of managing to construct an object that is much more aleatory than the one that might be made without live sound. (*Cahiers du Cinéma*, No. 223, 1970)

The driving sequences of *History Lessons* mark the first time Straub/Huillet applied this aleatory principle to the image-track in any extended manner (though the opening shot of *The Bridegroom, the Comedienne and the Pimp*, could be regarded in this way to an extent). Another moment that introduces the subject of «another film» occurs in the brief entry into frame of a woman in a turquoise dress, who is being followed by a man ... Similarly one can read the various traffic confrontations in narrative or metaphorical terms — «our» automobile giving way to others, squeezing past, surging forward; the drive is yielding, hesitant, aggressive by turns. Or there is the joyous instant when a group of youths on cycles erupt into the frame.

Although there is no fixed signification, there are many *signs,* once we begin to see (as opposed to receive) the drive. But these signs are in a process of drifting, unanchored, in the sense that it is exactly up to us, the viewers, to *produce* moments of stasis, to pluck a sign out of this magnificent sequence of flux and give that sign a tentative meaning, value. That is, in following this drive through a city we create meanings by disengaging elements from the perpetual shifting both of the drive through the city, and the light shifting across the screen. (Here, immediately, two arenas of meaning, the real world represented, and flatness of the image). We construct a reading. To cite Benjamin again:

> *Materialist historiography is based on a constructive principle. Thinking involves not only the flow of thoughts, but their arrest as well.*

We are not, in the car sequences, presented with a production, but must ourselves produce through disengaging elements from the drive, thereby privileging them, assigning them significant status.

We might here recall Barthes' observations on the contemporary convergence of the activities of reading and writing. The car sequence clearly poses the issue: we realise that the activity of reading is itself a a writing — as opposed to a reading of what is *already* written, in the sense that *Citizen Kane* is written, fixed in its significations. This convergence is also symptomatic of Straub/Huillet's cinematic praxis. All of their films are concerned with pre-existing texts (or in the case of *Introduction to Arnold Schoenberg's «Accompaniment for a Cinematographic Scene»*, a series of disparate texts, or documents). Böll, Bach, Bruckner, Corneille, Brecht, Schoenberg: upon the work of these have Straub/Huillet founded their own. (And an article they published in *Cahiers du Cinéma* consisted of answers to an Italian questionnaire, a French translation of a passage by Eisenstein, and, side by side, German and French versions of a passage by Brecht.) In every case we may say that Straub/Huillet's work is both a presentation and a critique of its origin, whether it be the hyperbolic reduction of Bruckner's two-hour play *Krankheit der Jugend* to a skeletal 10 minutes for *Bridegroom* or the very faithful treatment of Schoenberg's *Moses and Aaron*. Their films are critical settings: *History Lessons* presents segments of Brecht's «fragment-novel» — thus valorising those they retain: the social, economic history stays, the anecdotal elements are eliminated. But it is the way in which that social, economic history is represented, set that is more important, in so far as it appears to be quite congruent with Brecht's own formal notions, unlike virtually every previous Brecht film (except *Kuhle Wampe*, Brecht's collaborative work with Slatan Dudow), from Pabst to Losey.

The formal organisation of *History Lessons,* like *Introduction to Schoenberg,* is characterised by a displacement of the narrator: a series of accounts are proffered, rather than a simple, unified truth. (One movement of Straub/Huillet's oeuvre is from the first-person narration of *Machorka-Muff* to the heterogeneous complex of documents that constitute *Introduction to Schoenberg*). In an interview after the making of *Othon*, Straub said, «What interests me more and more is diversity» — and the *range* of speaking styles in *Othon* demonstrated clearly what he meant: diversity, plurality, movement against homogeneity. Brecht's *The Business Deals of Mr Julius Caesar* is organised according to a montage principle that juxtaposes the accounts given of Caesar by various people who knew him, and the notebooks of one of Caesar's slaves. And as Stephen Heath has pointed out, «Brecht declares his own point of view to lie in the montage, that is, in the undercutting of the young man's vision of history as the will of great men by a multiple focus on the economic and political determinations operative in Caesar's rise». In other words, it is the formal structural aspect that is crucial; only in (through) that, can we specify Brecht's stance. This common formal emphasis marks a decisive point of intersection between Brecht and Straub/Huillet.

For Straub/Huillet's formal decisions (particularly with respect to camera placement) are designed to ensure that the undercutting of the «young man's vision of history» is maintained in *History Lessons:* and this they achieve by refusing to place the audience in a situation of identification with the young man, by only rarely making *our* point of view that of the young man. This is in

Figure 1 Overhead diagram of shots 6 to 13.

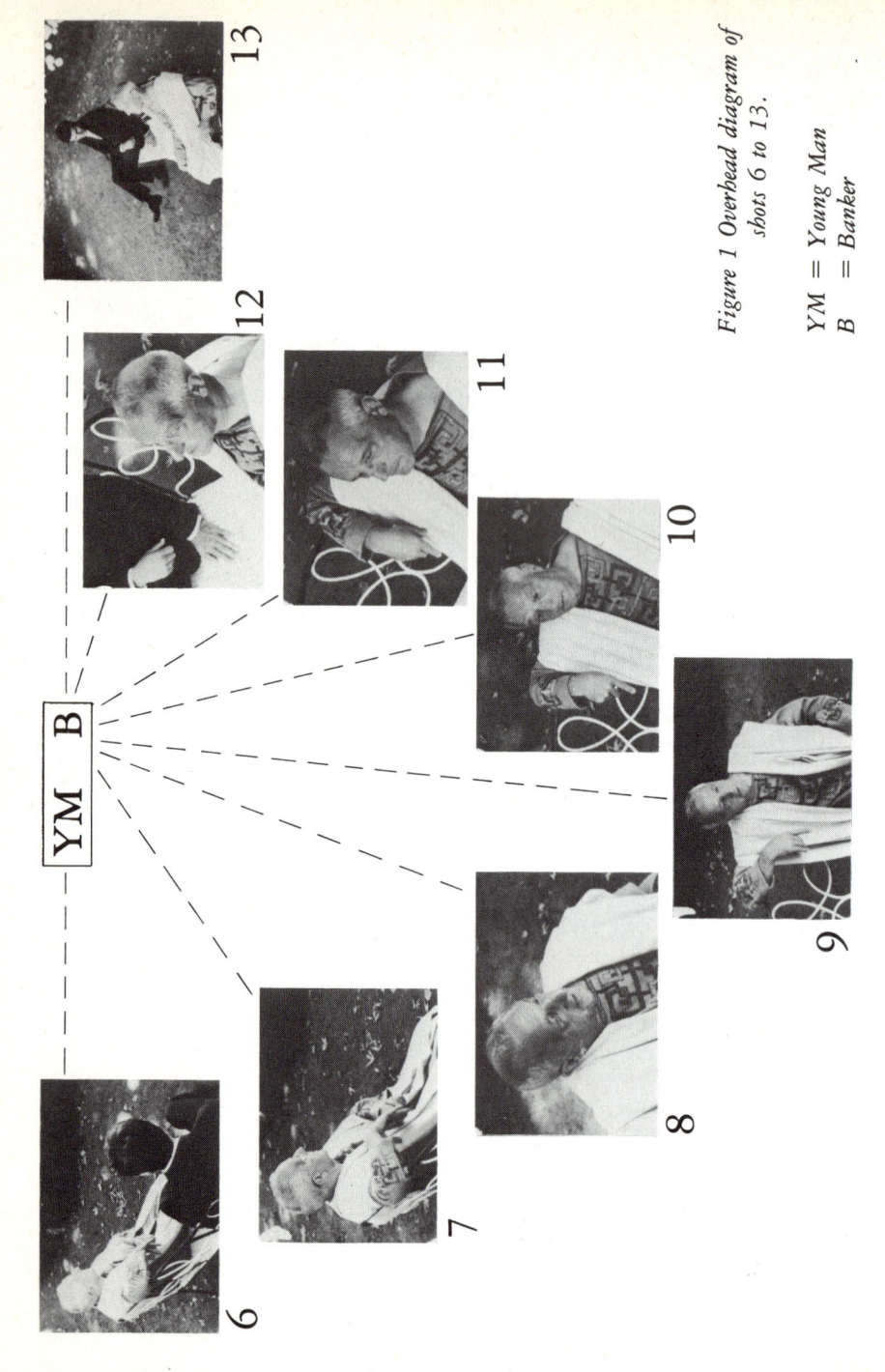

YM = Young Man
B = Banker

distinct contrast to a film such as *Citizen Kane,* which also makes use of a system of dispersed narration, and a constant interviewer. For in *Citizen Kane* the various accounts persistently overlap, repeat each other, thus establishing the «single, real and overflowing world» so beloved by Bazin. In *History Lessons* Straub/Huillet meticulously avoid any such *fixing* of the position of the spectator, as is made absolutely clear in the first sequence with the Banker. The sequence consists of 8 shots (numbers 6 to 13), the first of which is a high medium shot, from the side, looking down on the young man listening to the banker; after six seconds, this two-shot is cut, to be replaced by a medium close-up on the banker — and it should be remarked that this is, I think, the only «transparent» cut in the whole film: it appears to be on the same axis of orientation, composition, and both the banker's position (see his hands, for instance), and the angle he holds his head at, remain unchanged from shot 6 to shot 7. Shots 7 — 11 all frame only the banker, and last over seven minutes in total. Throughout this time the banker's gaze has been directed forward, *not* towards the young man who is at his side; and in the course of seven minutes we are apt to forget the establishing two-shot at the opening of the sequence, and assume the banker is addressing a person in front of him. Shot 12, however, still from a high angle, but turned nearly 180° from shot 6, reintroduces the young man's side and hands into the frame, and shot 13 is a two-shot that counterbalances shot 6. In fact there is a point, during shot 10, in which the banker addresses an «aside» to the young man, and it seems as if a third presence is added to the scene — since we assume the banker has been speaking to *someone*, situated as the object of his gaze through the bulk of his speech. For we are not the object of his gaze: our viewpoint is a very strange one, lacking any of the customary narrative logic of camera placement. Rather, the sequence of shots — as the symmetry between shots 6 and 13 suggests — is organised in a purely formal way, enclosing the banker's speech. The camera, in the space of 8 shots, describes a semi-circle around the bench on which the young man and the banker are seated. Shots 6 and 13 are two-shots, at either end of the 180° span, and other pairs are formed by 7/12, 8/11, 9/10 — pairs in respect of their axis of orientation to the banker; the distance from the subject is not matched (10 is closer to the banker than 9, for instance). These pairs are not *identical* shots, but exist in dialectical relationship to each other (see Fig. 1).

To understand the purpose of this structuring, let me quote from Barthes' essay «Brecht, Diderot, Eisenstein»:

> Brecht indicated clearly that in epic theatre . . . all the burden of meaning and pleasure bears on each scene, not on the whole. At the level of the play itself, there is no development, no maturation . . . there is no final meaning, nothing but a series of segmentations, each of which possesses a sufficient demonstrative power. (Barthes, 1974, p.35)

Straub/Huillet respect Brecht's segmentation of the text, and support it primarily through their editing strategies, which deny any sense of narrative development or interpretation of the verbal text: rather, each sequence is closed in on itself, defines its boundaries, its fundamental separation from the rest of the film, in accordance with Brecht's episodic theories. Thus we can quickly divide up the film's 55 shots (60 if we include 5 sections of black leader) into a series of self-sufficient segments established by the verbal text. Briefly, the film can be broken up in this manner:

Shot		
	1-3	*Map*
	4	*Statue*
	5	*Driving sequence*
	6-13	*Banker's speech*
	14/15	*Young man's first words, and exchange with banker*
	16	*Young man walking, reciting «official» Caesar and Pirates story*
	17-19	*The banker's version of Caesar and Pirates story*
	20-26	*20 is young man's question, 21-26 the banker's reply (with 5 sections of black leader between 21 and 26).*
	27-37	*Interview with the peasant, framed at beginning and end by the stream.*
	38	*Driving sequence*
	39-41	*Lawyer's speech*
	42-44	*Poet's speech, bracketed by shots of the sea (42 and 44)*
	45	*Driving sequence*
	46-53	*Banker's speech*
	54	*Banker's conclusion about Caesar («My confidence in him had proven well-founded. Our small bank was no small bank any more.»)*
	55	*The spewing fountain.*

A thorough analysis of the film would reveal this scheme to be flawed in certain respects — there is a variety of ways, for instance, of dividing up shots 17-26: I have here followed the one delineated by the narrative structure of Brecht's text, but it could be argued that formally interesting relations exist between shots 19/20/21, in terms of work upon the notion of reverse-field shooting. In other words, there are points at which there are obviously two (at least) levels upon which we may base our reading of the film, neither having any direct relation to the other.

This is important to recognise, since although Straub/Huillet's editing strategies respect Brecht's segmentation, those strategies in no sense themselves support the *content* of the segments. There is no homogenisation of the filmic elements to make possible a transparent reading of the verbal text. Rather, the formal organisation of each sequence is an explicitly materialist one which, more then simply «drawing attention to itself», is involved with an exploration of the parameters of classical narrative forms, by means of a systematic dismantling of those forms. We may say, at the same time, that this exploration is also concerned with a suspension of meaning, in the way indicated by Barthes:

> ... to create meaning is very easy, our whole mass culture elaborates meaning all day long; to suspend meaning is already an infinitely more complicated enterprise – it is an «art». (op. cit., p.272)

In the arena of cinematic language, *History Lessons* achieves just such a «suspension of meaning» by means of its separation of verbal text/filmic structure. Straub/Huillet's editing tactics delimit, segment, the verbal text, but do not *express* it: rather, each segment is organised quite systematically, but in terms of heterogeniety rather than homogeneity. Colin MacCabe has spoken of the contemporary necessity of dissolving homogeneity/belief into heterogeneity/knowledge (which is partly to point toward the recognition of contradiction, difference) and Straub/Huillet's textual organisation is devoted exactly to this end. But the knowledge they are concerned with is not that of the signified (the demythologisation of Caesar – that is Brecht's task) but rather with that of the signifier: their articulation of the filmic elements is designed to make explicit the arbitrary nature of those elements, signs. Cinematic language for them is not natural, innocent, self-effacing, transparent, but arbitrary, ideological, materialist.

Let us turn back again to the banker's first speech, shots 6–13, to see some of the ways in which this materialist approach is manifested.* I have already mentioned the way in which there is minimal eye-contact between the young man and the banker, and the way in which *our* point of view is separate from both characters, and is determined by the formal semi-circling of the scene by the camera in an 8-shot sequence. That is to say, there is an indeterminacy, a gap, between camera, actors, and audience – unlike the forms of classical narrative, there is no unifying thrust, no binding of these levels, elements. (It is perhaps worth observing that apart from throwing us back to our own situation as viewers, receivers, analysts, the lack of inter-personal connections – in a naturalist psychologising manner – re-engages the distance between Caesar's Rome/Modern Rome.) Each cut is also deliberately marked, after the near «transparent» or «invisible» editing of the transition from shot 6 to 7. This is primarily achieved through work on the soundtrack. The cut from shot 7 to 8 is emphatic in its sound elision – the cut comes between sentences, but eliminates the «natural» pause between them that we expect. Also the change

*For the scenario of *History Lessons*, see *Screen* vol. 17, no. 1, pp.54–76. However, where I quote from the film's speeches, I have used the English subtitles, rather than the published scenario (which appeared after this article was written).

in sound *quality* clearly points out that this is a new take — Straub/Huillet consistently refuse to equalise the soundtrack's tonal qualities prior to striking the master-negative. Hence the materiality of the cut is emphasised both by the diegetically unmotivated change of camera position (a 45° shift toward a frontal axis of orientation), and the foregrounded sound transition. The shift between shots 9 and 10 violates the classical «180° rule», in so far as in shot 9, the banker's gaze passes to the right (and underneath) the camera, while in shot 10 his gaze passes to the left. Further, the cut from 9 to 10 comes hard on the final word of the banker's sentence, which haste is then belied by the leisurely silence that occurs in shot 10 before the banker resumes speaking. The cut from shot 10 to 11 occurs balanced between two pauses — an aural equilibrium that the transition from 9 to 10 did not have. The cut from 11 to 12 investigates the tension between continuity and discontinuity in yet another manner; on the cut (i.e. at the end of 11 and beginning of 12), the banker moves his hand down through the frame, creating a sense of continuity that is at the same time challenged by the distinct change in sound quality.

In short, we may say that the materiality of each shot is stressed through a variety of tactics; the beginnings and endings of shots are strongly marked through shifts in sound quality between takes, through varying lengths of pause before words are spoken, through a systematic of camera angles that is unrelated to diegetic concerns (though it is worth observing that the young man and the banker sit together at the beginning of *History Lessons* and move subsequently further apart thereafter — thus «expressing» the young man's mounting rage). Further, we must note, within each shot, the mode of the actors' delivery — particularly that of the banker. For he clearly indicates that he is *quoting* — no naturalistic performance here — and throughout the film the banker's Brechtian delivery is of considerable importance in pursuing an anti-illusionist articulation. At one point, for instance, he makes it evident that he is *remembering* his lines, as opposed to recalling real events from his memory. At another moment he gazes silently past the camera (shot 26) for some twenty seconds, unblinking: here there is no *meaning,* simply a sense of the distance between the Rome he represents and his actual situation in the present; our thoughts are refocused again on his actorly status — we cease to view him as the banker. The fundamental contradiction involved in the attempt to represent a Roman banker is never glossed over, but rather underlined. Another way Straub/Huillet achieve this is through a high angle shot down onto the banker that reveals the contradiction banker/actor, since his tanned face is not matched by tanned shoulders, as would be the case if he customarily wore a toga.

In this respect Straub/Huillet seem close to Barthes' awareness of «The Diseases of the Costume»:

> . . . *epidemic ravages of the veristic malady in bourgeois art: costume, conceived as an*

accumulation of true details, absorbs then atomises the spectator's entire attention. (ibid., p.43)

Unlike Rossellini's historical films, Straub/Huillet's approach to costuming underlines its token nature: the first sequence with the banker which poses a modern dark suit against the toga, and the simple distinctions made between the banker, lawyer and poet through the type of embroidery that decorates their togas (the poet having a floral pattern, for instance), mark the limits of the attention paid to costume: it is economical, functional attention that finds no space for ornamentation. Similarly, when the banker sips a glass of wine, it is done not as a «natural» action, but as a sign pregnant with social meaning, marking the comfort of the patrician classes. This kind of gesticity characterises the performances throughout the film, and is eminently a Brechtian strategy, but frequently the function of such gestic moments is aimed not merely at a social situation, but at the materialist base of the film. Shot 20 is a good example: the young man is seated, and a leaf blows onto his arm, which he removes with an ironic smile, and pauses before speaking — it's a very ambiguous movement, we don't know whether it's improvised or planned, but either way we become strongly aware of the young man's performance of a role — his status as an actor who *quotes,* rather than identifying with his role, is explicit. Or again, Straub/Huillet's placing of the Poet in a deckchair assumes a gestic force — the posing of ancient against modern, and the implication of «the easy life» that is appropriate to his middle-class cynicism.

But while the actors' mode of delivery, the comparatively minimal use of the background of the frame for information (one exception occurs near the end: when the line «And the mountain valleys resound today with the peaceful hammering in the metal pits and with the merry call of the slaves» is delivered by the banker, Straub/Huillet cut to a shot (52) which situates the banker against a mansion, which specifically places him as a patrician), the sparse use of costume detail, the occasional decentring of the frame (as in shot 14, when the young man is situated on the right-hand side of the frame, and looks out right, instead of left across the empty space, which is the classic narrative way of maintaining a compositional balance), and so on, is important to the film's total mode of operation, it is nevertheless Straub/Huillet's structuring of each sequence of the film that is of paramount interest.

One reason for this is the extraordinary lack of repetition: as against the unifying repetitions of classical narrative, *History Lessons* never allows any solidification of its forms to occur, and every segment is organised according to a particular logic of its own. We have looked in some detail at shots 6 to 13, but we could equally take almost any segment for fruitful consideration. The constant factors may be described as an *enclosing* of each sequence through a symmetric sequence of shots (but never is any one symmetry repeated), and, within each sequence, an exploration of the tensions between continuity/discontinuity, transparency/opacity, through the constantly varying articulation of these tensions through modulation of camera angle, height, sound, silence, composition, posture, and so on. Shots 14 and 15, for instance, seem to be shot and reverse shot, but this is subverted by a difference in camera height. Shots 39/40/41 and 42/43/44 (the lawyer's speech, and the poet's) are formally paired, 40 and 43 both being bracketed, but in very different ways: 39 and 41 match compositionally (they are long shots of the lawyer, enclosing a medium close-up of him (40). 42 and 44 are both shots from the sea, of the poet's house bracketing the poet's speech, 43. There is then, a constant awareness of sameness and difference, of formal matching on some levels, but not others.

Three sections in particular deserve brief analysis. Shots 21 to 26, 27 to 37, and 46 to 53 are each organised in a beautiful and complex manner. Shots 21 to 26 constitute a formal unit articulated through the use of a series of black segments between shots. The first striking fact is that, in contrast to every other section of the film, each of the 6 shots, 21 to 26, is compositionally identical, but the discreteness of each shot is emphasised both by the interpolation of the black leader, and by changes in light (and hence colour) quality, in the banker's posture, in the sound quality, and in the rhythm and pacing of the sound transitions. The length of black leader varies, but is itself systematised: 6 or 7 frames between shots 21/22 and 25/26, 15 frames between shots 22/23 and 24/25, and 24 frames between shots 23/24: the symmetry is self-evident, the length of black leader being greatest between the two middle shots. This formal structure loses its apparent rigidity through its interaction with the other variables of the sequence: words spurt out from the very first moment of shot 22, while in shot 23 the banker has inclined his head slightly, revealing a red flower in the bush behind him, and at the end of the take the Banker's words carry over into the black leader. The transition from 24 to 25 is more nearly «transparent», in so far as the sound pause is quite naturalistic, as if the speech runs smoothly on, and there is hardly any shift in the sound quality — but the light quality is different, and marks the fact that this *is* a new take. And at the end of 26, the banker sits silent for 20 seconds, marking the end of his speech, but also, as already mentioned, pointing to more complex relations between past/present, acting/being, and so on. So despite the superficially sterile formalism of the organisation of the black spaces, the effect of the sequence as a whole is much more complex and rewarding than accusations of «formalism» would lead us to believe.

Shots 27 to 37 embrace the young man's interview with the peasant, and the interview is framed at either end by a close-shot of a stream rushing by. Following the long immobile silence of the banker in shot 26, the noise and vigour of the stream is a very abrupt inauguration of the next segment. Beginning with a close-up of the stream, the camera pans left, to look up the valley towards the mountain: we can see the young man and the peasant standing by a hut in the distance. Shot 28 is a lateral medium close-up of the peasant, looking out frame left, and shot 29 is a frontal close-up of the young man, his gaze passing right of the camera. The next 6 shots elaborate a kind of intertwined circling of the two men, in a series of shot and reverse shots «manqué»: that is to say the camera's placement does not fulfil the demands of the shot and reverse form, although the alternating shots, from peasant to young man and back again, do. Throughout the sequence, the camera's axis of orientation upon the young man is at a 90° difference from that upon the peasant: see Fig. 2.

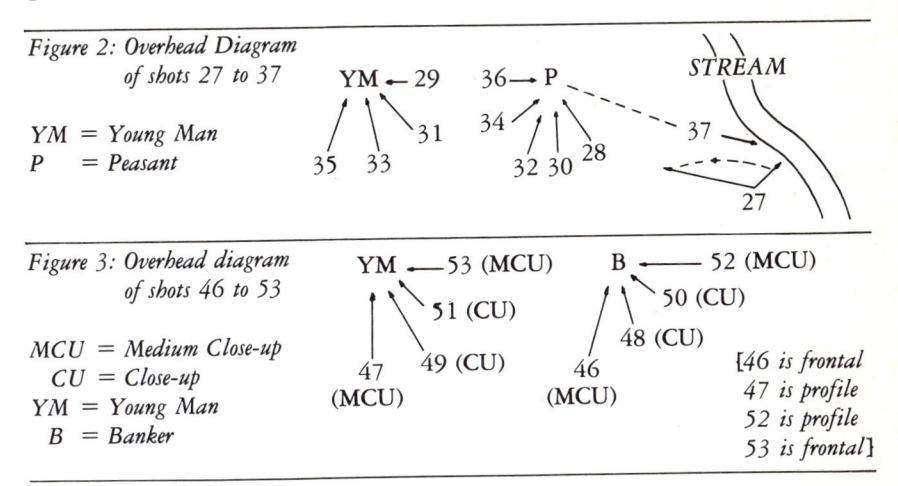

Figure 2: Overhead Diagram of shots 27 to 37

YM = Young Man
P = Peasant

Figure 3: Overhead diagram of shots 46 to 53

MCU = Medium Close-up
CU = Close-up
YM = Young Man
B = Banker

[46 is frontal
47 is profile
52 is profile
53 is frontal]

Although they face each other, the camera placement subverts this apparent contact, and we have to perceive the choice of angles and the system of editing as, once again, not supporting the dialogue that is taking place, but as performing its own enclosing choreography of the episode – the twin circling (i.e. shots 29, 31, 33, 35, describe an arc around the young man, and shots 28, 30, 32, 34, 36, describe an arc around the peasant and the last shot [35] on the young man is in the same direction as the first shot on the peasant [28]), enables the camera at the end of this movement (shot 36) to be framing not only the peasant, but, in the background, the stream which opened the sequence – and shot 37 symmetrically closes the section by returning to a close shot of the rushing water.

It is worth noticing that the camera pans up the stream – against the flow, as if fighting to regain a lost point of origin, a source for our present, the very theme of history. And this water image is taken up again, in the two shots taken from a boat at sea, bracketing the poet's speech, and again in the film's close, in the image of the fountain's face spewing water. It is perhaps not irrelevant to allude to Lautréamont's *Chants de Maldoror,* whose figures of the «ocean» Stephen Heath has described as the

> *perfect analogue of the text itself, ceaseless movement of construction and deconstruction never fixed but in the destruction of itself.* (Heath, 1972, p.38)

For *History Lessons* is concerned precisely with this «ceaseless movement of construction and deconstruction», and both the images of water with their ceaseless flow, and the driving sequences (no ground is repeated across the three drives) underpin this notion with their effective power (particularly the stream and the fountain) which resists reduction to any precise single meaning. Indeed there are interesting analogies to be made between the formal operations of *History Lessons,* and a poem, called «wave» by Scottish concrete poet Ian Hamilton Finlay:

\wae \v wv \ae a \vwe \wave

The analogy between language and ocean is here explicit — and of course the wave forms only to break immediately thereafter. The sinuous curve/wave that segments the letters signifies the movement of a wave, while simultaneously recalling Hogarth's line of beauty. The interplay between the triple and quadruple groupings of the letters, and the symmetry of the second and third triads, «v wv» and «ae a», seem not very remote from the structures built by Straub/Huillet in *History Lessons,* their constant play on cinematic language, their avoidance of a fixed, permanent codification of cinematic elements.

The last formally sustained sequence of *History Lessons* occurs in shots 46 to 53, and its operation resembles that of shots 27 to 37, except that here we don't have the 90° displacement of camera angle between the young man and the peasant. Now, in contrast to the banker's visual domination of shots 6 to 13, we have a contrapuntal visual organisation (see Fig. 3), alternating between the young man and the banker: shots 46, 48, 50, and 52 are on the banker, while shots 47, 49, 51, 53 are on the young man: 46, 47, 52 and 53, are medium close-ups, while 48, 49, 50, 51 are close-ups. This symmetry is crossed by another, however: shot 46 is frontal on the banker, shot 47 is profile on the young man, and at the end of the sequence this is reversed, so that shot 52 is profile on the banker and 53 is frontal on the young man. This occurs due to the fact that the young man is sitting at a 90° angle to the banker, not to a difference in the camera's axis of orientation, as was the case in shots 27 to 37. The camera *is* displaced laterally however — about 4 feet separates the axes of orientation of the camera for each man — but they remain parallel in their quarter-circling of the actors, and we get a series of *paired* shots: 46/47, 48/49, 50/51, 52/53. So again we read two (at least) texts — Brecht's verbal one, and Straub/Huillet's formal one, the two co-existing, interdependent in fundamental ways, yet neither subjugating the other. Straub/Huillet have respected Brecht's dictum that cinema is «by nature static, and must be treated as a succession of *tableaux*», and yet in the structuring of these *tableaux* they have managed to pursue a cinematic project of extraordinary interest and beauty.

Noël Burch has described

a set of formal «objects» — the 15 different types of shot transition and the parameters that define them — capable of rigorous development through such devices as rhythmic alternation, recapitulation, retrogression, gradual elimination, cyclical repetition and serial variation, thus creating structures similar to those of twelve-tone music. (Burch, 1973, p.14)

Straub/Huillet's next project, significantly, was Schoenberg's *Moses and Aaron*; and their reconstruction of the potentials of cinematic language may perhaps be seen in parallel to Schoenberg's rebuilding of the systems of musical thought that had dominated nineteenth-century composition. Certainly the kind of formal investigations undertaken in *History Lessons* extends the possibilities Burch outlines quite considerably, and seems, in contrast to a text of *«plaisir»*, like *Citizen Kane* (to use the token classical text already cited), to mark *History Lessons* as clearly a text of *«jouissance»*. As Barthes has written:

the subject gains access to bliss (jouissance) *by the cohabitation of languages working side by side.* (Barthes, 1975, p.4)

The achievement of *History Lessons* is precisely the manner in which no one language dominates any other, the way in which the spectator is given room to construct his own reading, to work at a plurality of possible meanings. The analysis undertaken in these pages does not presume to be complete, of course, rather to suggest certain ways of formulating the relation that exists between Brecht and Straub/Huillet. For it is rare to find a film of a Brecht text that is not subverted by precisely the kind of homogenisation that underlay Brecht's «fundamental reproach» to cinema: in *History Lessons,* however, we are not confronted with «a production produced in our absence», but must engage in the activity of producing a reading, largely through our encounter with Straub/Huillet's materialist play on, subversion of, the codes of acting, lighting, continuity, sound, editing rhythm, camera placement and so on. Just as Brecht liberates us from the normative image of Caesar, so Straub/Huillet free us from the visual/aural chains of cinematic illusionism, thereby enacting Barthes' dictum that

Whosoever wants to write with exactitude must . . . proceed to the frontiers of language. (op. cit., p.xv)

This article originally appeared as « ‹History Lessons› : Brecht and Straub/Huillet: The Frontiers of Language» in *Afterimage,* No. 7, Spring 1977, and is published here in an abridged version by kind permission.

«Introduction to Arnold Schoenberg's ‹Accompaniment for a Cinematographic Scene›»

Certain elements of culture are common to both classes. Certainly we must maintain that some habitual elements of culture have played out their role, and are become elements of unculture. But there are other elements that remain which are in difficulty and which we need to defend . . . To take over culture means to transform it decisively.

Bertolt Brecht

Pleasure of the text. Classics. Culture. Intelligence. Irony. Delicacy. Euphoria. Mastery. Security: art of living. Texts of pleasure. *Pleasure in pieces; language in pieces; culture in pieces.*

Roland Barthes

Straub and Huillet's *Introduction to Arnold Schoenberg's «Accompaniment for a Cinematographic Scene»* (henceforth referred to as *Introduction*) marks a decisive intervention in the arena of the relations between music and politics, working from the specific position of a short television documentary about a single piece of music. In Edinburgh, August 1975, Straub/Huillet sketched out the origins and context of the project:

> *The film was commissioned by the 3rd channel of German television. The Germans had two other films, one made by Jan Mortenson, a Swedish musician, another by a young Frenchman, Luc Ferrari, two very different films to ours, absolutely a-political, on the same piece of music. We had an agreement that our film would be shown last, if it was put on at all (because there was a risk it would not be: but if it hadn't been, well, we had the negative, we'd made the film, and we could have shown it elsewhere).*
>
> *Introduction is directed to the most restricted audience of all the films we have made, because it was directed to the audience which regularly listens to this programme, a half-hour programme on new experimental music and film, which is put out once or twice a month, very late, around 10.30 or 11 p.m., to people who never talk politics, for whom it doesn't exist.* (Straub/Huillet, 1976)

This then, is the context of the attempt to «take over culture», as Brecht put it, an attempt that is articulated in *Introduction* through work on dominant assumptions about both music *and* films. Both in terms of their approach to Schoenberg, to the «Accompaniment for a Cinematographic Scene», and to the structure of a television documentary, Straub/Huillet reveal «culture in pieces»: which is to say, «in pieces» from the point of view of the culture-mongers, of those for whom art functions toward the entrenchment of the «status quo», from the point of view, in short, of those for whom reinforcement rather than change is the proper aim of aesthetic endeavour.

I have not seen the two films that Straub/Huillet's followed, but given the information quoted above, it seems reasonable to assume they followed a

Arnold Schoenberg

certain orthodoxy of such works: a textual «appreciation», perhaps marking the «high points» of «Accompaniment»; or a chat about twelve-tone composition, using this film as illustrative material; or perhaps they followed a biographical course — the tortured genius holding stage-front against a background of musical dismissal and scorn, with «Accompaniment» thus constituting his cry of «universal anguish»; if a political angle is mentioned at all, it would be diminished by the partiality of its recognition, or generalised into a European fear of the Nazis; and the audience would be given the security of a historical distance which simply affirms that «we know better today, but what a pity the great artists couldn't work unharried by such political pressures».

It is of course precisely on the basis of this argument that Schoenberg attacks Kandinsky in the two letters read in *Introduction*: Schoenberg refuses to be extracted from his history, the fact of his being Jewish is not something he will have conveniently erased. Nor, Straub/Huillet suggest, is the barbarous world of politics, war and the law to be detached from consideration of the aesthetic object. «Accompaniment» came out of a specific social context, and its heading «Threatening Danger, Fear, Catastrophe» is accessible not only to the universalist, expressionist reading that has been the usual approach, but to the *specific* pressures upon his material, physical life. But Straub/Huillet are not principally interested in these biographical dimensions; rather, the two letters to Kandinsky are presented in a conjuncture with materials of very different origins — a quotation from Brecht, some news/archive footage, images from a newspaper report — their very diversity drawing us away from immersion in the *personal* drama of Schoenberg, the man.

The quotation from Brecht (from his address to the «1935 Paris Congress of Intellectuals Against Fascism») points to the relation between fascism and capitalism, a relation that must be acknowledged if fascism is to be actively confronted — underlining that «Accompaniment» must be seen in relation to the conditions which led to its articulation. Similarly the archival footage of mass murder victims neatly lined up in trim coffins (they are not Nazi ones, but victims of Monsieur Thiers, in Paris 1871 — in Straub's view the first mass murder victims of modern capitalism) is then explicated in terms not only of aircraft bombing, but of the making of the bombs in the factory and the loading of the bombs onto the planes. All stages of the process are equally responsible for the murders. This theme recurs in the final section, the newspaper article:

> *Concentration camp architects acquitted . . . The principal questions, whether the two accused were guilty of participation in mass murder through having drawn up plans for gas chambers and crematories, were unanimously answered in the negative.*

Thus the film ends on a note of reactionary closing: the newspaper's report is not our own, however, and the total movement of the film throws us hard in denial against the court decision. We are impelled to deny the force of law, a denial that finds its echo in a phrase of Schoenberg's in the second letter to Kandinsky, to the effect that «official talk is all lies». The force of law, the offices of authority (both social and linguistic): this is the arena that Straub/Huillet, Brecht and Schoenberg are commonly concerned to confront, subvert, deconstruct. All are concerned, as was said of Brecht, with «clearing rubble out of brains»; it is the attack upon cultural institutions, assumptions and valuations that is fundamental to their activities.

And yet Schoenberg would never have admitted a view of his work which situated it as co-extensive with political activity. His hostility to politics is well-known — indeed Straub/Huillet have omitted one section from the second letter to Kandinsky, in which Schoenberg rails against the «rivers of blood» spilt by Lenin and Trotsky. In a letter written in Los Angeles in 1948,

Schoenberg (who on another occasion wrote, «If it is art, it is not for the masses») said:

> *We who live in* music *have no place in politics and must regard* [*politicians*] *as essentially something alien to us. We are apolitical and the most we can do is endeavour to stay quietly in the background.* (Schoenberg, 1964, p.255)

This conscious desire for total separation of music and politics is precisely opposed by Straub/Huillet's structuring of *Introduction.* Why do they take this unorthodox stand? Because they are reformulating a connection that Schoenberg himself *repressed,* but whose traces remain inscribed in the musical texture of «Accompaniment», as in most of his work. Theodor Adorno, in his seminal essay on Schoenberg in *Prisms,* has stated the issue lucidly: «Against his will, that which crystallised in his work embodied immanent musical opposition to [his] socially naïve conceptions.» (Adorno, 1967, p.171)*

Which is to say that Schoenberg as a composer functioned in a revolutionary manner: his aesthetics, his music, threaten and subvert the tenets of his musical antecedents. His verbal retreats from politics cannot bury his *musical* threat to the status quo. As he recognised early in his career, «The alleged tones believed to be foreign to harmony do not exist; they are merely foreign to our accepted harmonic system.» (Schoenberg, 1937, p.4) His rejection of the so-called «laws of harmony» marked his recognition that, in Barthes' phrase, «the text is (should be) that uninhibited person who shows his behind to the *Political Father*». The rejection of the constraints, rules, conventions of harmonic structures constitutes Schoenberg's direct attack upon the musical institutions that continued, even through his lifetime, to insist upon the inviolable universality of the musical language whose support was exactly the stock of assumptions dismantled by Schoenberg's practice as a composer.

Schoenberg's position was that the parameters of musical expression had become so atrophied by the close of the nineteenth-century, so limiting and determined, that only *parodies* of feelings could any longer be transmitted — only a palid *simulation* of emotion could be achieved, particularly through a form of music that was devoted to elegant transitions, tonal depth, and a smooth accessibility of surface: an aural texture without flaws, ruptures, roughness. Schoenberg's task was to renew musical language to the point whereby it became possible once more to explore «the pure elaboration of musical thoughts»: the possibility of this had been closed off during the nineteenth century in terms of *performance* practice as well as compositional mannerism. Not only were harmonics rigidly controlled in the exclusion of any alternative procedure, but all music was performed in «equal temperament». [. . .] Thus choral music of the late Mediaeval and Renaissance

---

*See also Adorno's *The Philosophy of Modern Music.*

periods, which was meant to be harmonised by acoustically correct concords, and the music of the seventeenth and eighteenth centuries, which was meant to be heard in the changing key-coloration of meantone, was denied its historical specificity, and musically «generalised» into «equal temperament». In short, the historical specificity of pre-nineteenth-century music is repressed by an ideological manipulation which gives credence to the notion of «eternal» music, precisely through the standardisation of methods of tuning.

In his attempt to regain a grasp upon musical specificity, Schoenberg may be seen to be close to Barthes' notion that «the whole task of art is to unexpress the expressible»: «the expressible» being that sanctioned meaning, the meanings made possible and contained by convention, by language in its socialised form. And society, as always, resists such endeavours. Schoenberg's current situation, both economically and critically, still suggests a social resistance to the acceptance of his musical ideas. Economically, it is necessary only to point out that there is no recording available at the present time of «Accompaniment». Of the two opera films released this year (1976), Bergman's *Magic Flute* (replete with an audience that comprises representatives of all nations, ages, sexes— such is the eternal universal appeal of Mozart!) has been accorded extensive exhibition, while Straub/Huillet's *Moses and Aaron* has received only single screenings. To say this is so because Bergman's film is «better» would be to sidestep the issue entirely. What is at issue here is *not* a question of «better» or «worse», but «acceptable» or «threatening». The conjunction of Bergman and Mozart is, in this respect, absolutely predictable, in so far as it slots into the mutually reinforcing cycle of «desire» (for universal art) and «satisfaction» that operates between industry, texts, and audience.

Between economics and criticism we must situate the rarity, even today, of concert performances of Schoenberg's work — a repression of the «nobody will come if we *do* perform this important music, and we'll be bankrupt» type. And on the critical side — well, Adorno's description will suffice us here:

> *In the public mind of today (1955) Schoenberg appears as an innovator, as a reformer, even as the inventor of a system. With grudging respect it is admitted that he prepared the way for others, a way, it is true, which they had no great desire to travel; yet this concession is linked to the implication that he himself was a failure and has already become obsolete. The one-time pariah is repressed, neutralised and absorbed.* (Adorno, op. cit. p.149)

This attitude remains prevalent: in a volume edited by the Marxist-Leninist composer and critic Cornelius Cardew, Rod Eley condemned «serialism, the tradition stemming from Schoenberg», as «formal, abstract and authoritarian», «élitist, uncompromisingly bourgeois and anti-people». (Eley, 1974, p. 12) Schoenberg is unjustly accused of an impotent adherence to the twelve-tone system, as if he composed by rote: as Schoenberg insisted in a letter to a pupil in 1932, «my works are twelve note *compositions*, not *twelve note* compositions». (op. cit., pp. 164–5) But still the critical orthodoxy reduces Schoenberg's music to a product of the intellect that ignored emotion (again the idealist dichotomy), and consistently minimises the extent of his break not just from compositional principles dominant in the nineteenth century, but from several centuries of musical tradition.

And it is this break from several hundred years of musical practice that is perhaps of central concern here in so far as it connects to the intervention undertaken by both Brecht and Straub/Huillet in the fields of theatrical and cinematic praxis. In cinema, Straub/Huillet, along with Godard, Vertov and others, pursue the ramifications of their break with traditions of narrative, visual codicity, and «illusionism». The terms of this departure are in many respects parallel to those of Schoenberg's work: for instance, the elimination of perspectival illusionism (Bazin's depth of reality) that is so crucial to Straub/Huillet and Godard finds its echo in Schoenberg's elimination of tonal harmony – the tonal, «spatial» harmony that gives the aural illusion of spatial depth, volume. Similarly, as Adorno has pointed out, «contrast, repressed in the nineteenth century by transition, becomes the formative technique» (op. cit., p. 154) – contrast providing some kind of a match with the emphasis upon montage reappears throughout Brecht and Straub/Huillet. The «separation of elements», a materialist articulation that resists homogenisation – and hence resists the appeal to any single, universal «truth» – is common to Straub/Huillet and Brecht, as it is to Schoenberg.

In this respect it is instructive to see how Adorno's description of Schoenberg could almost be transposed to one of Straub/Huillet:

Such repression . . . is provoked by the difficulties that Schoenberg poses to a listening public that has been kneaded into shape by the culture industry. (ibid., p. 149)

With Schoenberg, affability ceases . . . He sins against the division of life into work and leisure . . . His passion points to a music of which the mind need not be ashamed . . . (ibid., p. 150)

Schoenberg's intolerance of all excess ornaments stems from generosity, from his reluctance to have the listener deprived of true riches by ostentation. (ibid., p. 151)

Ordering categories, which reduce the difficulties of active listening at the cost of the pure elaboration of the work, are eliminated. (ibid., p. 153)

Indeed these words of Adorno's recollect certain ideas of Brecht as much as those of Straub/Huillet, and before talking more extensively about specific aspects of *Introduction*, it is perhaps useful to sketch out Brecht's situation in this conjunction of minds. For the overt place of Brecht within *Introduction* is not large. He is quoted, to be sure, on two occasions: the first in a purely visual quotation as, in the second shot of the film, Jean-Marie Straub lights his cigarette, in leisurely fashion, before speaking, alluding unmistakably to Brecht's emphasis on the constructive spectator's attitude of 'smoking-and-watching', on the necessity for an active, but detached spectator.

> *I even think that in a Shakespearean production one man in the stalls with a cigar could bring about the downfall of Western art. He might as well light a bomb as light a cigar.* (Brecht, 1964a, p.8).

The second quotation is a verbal one, split into two parts, the first recited by Danièle Huillet as she strokes the cat, and continued by the man in the recording studio. This is concerned with one of the film's thematic levels, as we have seen, and we might paraphrase its importance through a formulation of Brecht's friend, Walter Benjamin: «There is no document of civilisation which is not at the same time a document of barbarism». (Benjamin, 1969, p.256) The document of civilisation — i.e. the music — is at the same time the trace of barbarism, of anti-semitism: it is through the reference to Brecht that the relation between music as high art to be revered and mass murder, concentration camps, is clarified.

But there is a third level, and to my mind this is the crucial one, at which Brecht is vital to a reading of *Introduction:* that is that *Introduction* seems clearly Brechtian in the mode of its articulation, and constitutes a cinematic reformulation of certain Brechtian concepts. It is at this level, as I shall go on to show, that Brecht is crucial, rather than at the level of any *conscious* connection between Schoenberg and Brecht. Certainly the two men met — in Hollywood in 1942, ironically — via Hanns Eisler, Brecht's collaborator who was Schoenberg's pupil. One account records that

> *Schoenberg had no idea who Brecht was, and Brecht rejected the composer's music in a manner which a modern composer would think monstrous: «Schoenberg is too melodius for me, too sweet!»* (Eisler, 1975, p.94)

Brecht heard Schoenberg lecture and was impressed by his «utter clarity», but although Schoenberg later visited Brecht in the hope that they might try to write some new popular songs with «music in the new manner», the project never came to anything, and it is difficult to conceive of Schoenberg's hostility to the world of politics as ever allowing such a conjuncture to take place.

For a more general sense of the connection between Schoenberg and Brecht, we may turn back to the quotation from Brecht: «To take over culture means to transform it decisively.» Schoenberg does not desire to eradicate pre-Schoenbergian music, and his teaching and writing, as well as his own compositions, testify to the continuing importance of Bach and Brahms, for instance, in his musical thinking. It is in his process of transformation, his relocation of elements of earlier musical thinking, that Schoenberg recalls Brecht's ability to transform historical materials into uncompromisingly modern challenges to entrenched ways of thinking.

A kind of cipher of this «community of interest» (Brecht, Schoenberg, Straub/Huillet) can be found in their attitudes toward the cinema, film. One critic has spoken of Brecht's approach to the *The Life of Edward II* as «a fragile structure suspended in unrealistic space» (Reich, 1975, p.41), and this concentration upon a non-illusionist space is reiterated in Brecht's own conviction that cinema is «by nature static and must be treated as a succession of *tableaux*». In 1913, when it was proposed that Schoenberg's *Die glückliche Hand* might be filmed, Schoenberg was quite emphatic about his orientation: «My foremost wish is therefore for something the opposite of what the cinema generally aspires to: the utmost unreality». (Schoenberg, 1964, p.44) And, as Straub points out in *Introduction,* there are, in contrast to the thoroughness of his details for his stage works, no directions for «Accompaniment» beyond the heading «Threatening Danger, Fear, Catastrophe»: the scene is otherwise unimaginable, resists visualisation, will not allow its reality to be simply reproduced upon the screen. Only forty years later is it possible for the «Accompaniment for a Cinematographic Scene» to take its place within a cinematographic scene: Straub/Huillet being among the few film-makers to have a hold upon the kind of unreality envisaged by Schoenberg and Brecht. *Introduction* is indeed itself «a fragile structure suspended in unrealistic space», and it would not be inaccurate to say that its desire is to reach «something the opposite of what cinema usually aspires to».

I have already suggested that the enterprise of *Introduction* [. . .] challenges one's expectations of a television documentary on modern music. [. . .] Indeed, *Introduction* is deconstructive of cinematic language, particularly in the way it takes a materialist, as opposed to idealist, stance toward the notion of the documentary. Straub/Huillet do not attempt to find footage of Schoenberg as a young man, nor do they seek out «live» reminiscences by his friends, nor is there any attempt to reconstruct the «Accompaniment's» musical background, its placing in his total *oeuvre*. And the reason this path is ignored is that such a presentation would result in a reimposition of the normative «cultured» view of Schoenberg, and it would, at the same time, result in a «fixing-in-position» of the spectator, who would be given knowledge about the individual genius Schoenberg, and thus placed in the position of the consumer, as opposed to the more active role Straub/Huillet assign us.

Perhaps the first thing to be noted about the structure of *Introduction* is its curious lack of a narrative centre, a line of thought or of identification which would allow the spectator to acquire a certain sense of passive security. Instead of «a narrator» to endow the film with a unity and authoritative consciousness,

Straub/Huillet disperse the role of narrator into a series of disconnected, autonomous segments: first Straub himself, then the man reading the letters, followed by Huillet quoting Brecht, which passage is then continued by another narrator in another unrelated setting. The oral narration is then abandoned, and two sections of «visual narration» follow — the bombing sequence and the newspaper article. The lack of any apparent relationship between these various narrative voices throws our position as *receivers* of the text into abeyance: our relationship to the film, our engagement with it, is implicitly interrogated.

Stephen Heath has suggested that the most obvious of all Brechtian emphases is exactly this destruction of the unity of identification. According to Brecht

the individual as spectator loses his epicentral role, and disappears; he is no longer a private person «present» at a spectacle organised by theatre people, appreciating a work which he has shown to him; he is no longer a simple consumer, he must also produce. (Heath, 1975, p.39)

It is, of course, not merely the multi-narrational structure that matches with Brechtian principles. While it does accomplish a certain distanciation, the total organisation of the film is equally devoted to a buttressing of this materialist stance. We might note a characteristic Straub/Huillet element such as the diagonal orientation of the camera, that thereby evades any eye-contact between narrator/spectator (except in the shot of Danièle Huillet, who speaks at the camera/spectator: yet even here their organisation of the frame functions to break that gaze, since the movement of the cat persistently attracts our eye). Or the «flat» delivery of the verbal texts that refocuses the ear upon the rhythms of language, as opposed to simply its meaning: the materiality of the spoken text is reasserted. Straub once said that «language is colonisation», referring to the «fixing of meaning», the solidification of signifier and signified into an identity, and it is precisely this solidification that is fought through the re-emphasis upon the musical and rhythmic attributes of language as it sounds, as it is spoken — as opposed to the *written* which appears in this film (as in *Machorka-Muff* and *Chronicle*) as a form of terrorisation. The themes of «the written» in these three films are rearmament, begging for money, concentration camps. This so-called «terrorisation» of language is countered, then, by Straub/Huillet's «unexpressing the expressible», in so far as the aural materiality, musicality of language is reasserted in the reading. In *Introduction*, the written text, the newspaper, is countered by the music of the «Accompaniment», and its force thereby diminished.

Indeed we might say that the battle between sound and image is one of the fundamental axes upon which the film operates. Thus *Introduction* parallels

Schoenberg's basic scheme for *Moses and Aaron*: speech vs. song, word vs. image, and equivocal oscillation. The film's process is a search to let *feeling* burst through the intransigent density of the letter — Schoenberg's music operates against the reading of the letters, of Brecht, of the newspaper. The sombre tone of the readings has a specificity that opens a new way of hearing the music, both as «fear», and as a *refusal* of fear and oppression, as a transcendent liberation from fear. The division of the figure of Schoenberg in *Introduction* into a verbal and musical presence (along with two photographs, and a self-portrait) is in one sense resolved, in so far as the film's movement is from the verbal to the musical, with a period of overlap in the middle of the film. The music's independence from, lack of synchronisation with, the verbal texts marks its aesthetic independence — its transcendent existence outside the realm of persecution. There are occasional (and crucial) points of coincidence and these moments are the more emphatic, thanks to their rarity. For instance, the musical eruption that coincides with the smoke that follows the explosion of the bombs raises once more the question of how we are to relate these apparently contradictory events, music and war.

A more general perspective upon the music's lack of synchronisation with the verbal text (the separation of elements in the Brechtian sense) marks a refusal of Hollywood's characteristic homogenisation of elements. Another element of this «deconstruction» may be seen in the despecularisation of the image track. For in the dominant narrative tradition the homogenisation of elements is directed not towards a *unity* that assigns equal importance to each channel of the discourse, but to supporting and strengthening the authority of the image-track. In other words, sound characteristically is used to ensure the «reality» of the image. It is this «reality», of course, that Brecht objected to in photography and cinema: «the simple ‹reproduction of reality› says nothing at all about that reality». (Heath, op. cit., p.35) Writing of this, Stephen Heath has noted that

> *for Brecht, the photograph is the sublimation of reality into passive ideality; hence his constant emphasis on the need for «literarisation», for the montage construction, operation of the photograph with language . . . A materialist practice of film must then in turn be inevitably involved in combat against the sublimation of film in the luminous reality-truth of the photograph . . .* (ibid., p.36)

In *Introduction* Straub/Huillet counter this sublimation by attacking the very grounds upon which the cinema has been said to be the perfection of photography: Straub/Huillet despecularise the image by minimising movement — the supposedly «essential» quality of cinema. That is to say, the images (with the necessary exception of the bombing sequence) have a still-photo quality; the motion-picture refinds stasis, a factor which makes precise the distinction between document and documentary. It is in Straub/Huillet's presentation of each sequence as a document, a fragment, a piece of celluloid material that the idealist notion of documentary is shredded. The ideology of the visible is further threatened by the evacuation of meaning from the images that precede the bombing sequence: we see people speaking, reading letters: and yet this vision tells us little: to see is not therefore to know.

What these images *do* tell us, each in its own way, is that everything in this film is quotation: «presentation-as-quotation» being, of course, one of Brecht's precepts for the actor in the theatre, since it helped achieve the alienation, estrangement of the audience from the actor's representation. In *Introduction* the notion of quotation is used in a variety of ways: Straub and Huillet both quote through reciting, respectively, Schoenberg and Brecht; the man who reads Kandinsky's letters, on the other hand, and the man who reads from Brecht, are both shown to be reading from a text in front of them; while the bombing sequence is clearly presented as quotation from newsreel archive, and acquittal of the concentration camp architects is presented as quotation from a newspaper. These series of quotations — which are closely related to the lack of a single «coherent» narrator discussed above — may be seen to be the «literarisation» of the text, a Brechtian implementation of montage that seeks not to smooth out the elements of the text into a single, unified statement, but to leave these points of rupture, contradiction as a crucial aspect of the text; the temporal dislocations, shifts between more than fifty years, are foregrounded, in the juxtaposition of colour and black and white, in the shifts from Schoenberg's words to Straub's representation of them, while the bomb sequence exists between, apart from these two poles. The «continual present-tense» of the cinematic experience is thus posed in terms of its contradictions.

In this respect it is worth quoting Straub's observation in Edinburgh, 1975, that

> *what . . . interests us in the films we make is to leave the various layers, not eliminating anything. This is the contrary of a whole Western artistic tradition, bourgeois of course, which consists in destroying, in effacing the traces and destroying these layers. There are other traditions . . . Brecht said, when asked what had marked him most, «Don't laugh, it was the Bible», and he of course meant the Lutheran translation. It's a question of epochs — instead of taking away, one adds; the things written 500 years earlier are not removed, they're left. In a film what interests us is the stratification, like in geology.* (Straub/Huillet, 1976, p.93)

Such stratification is what most film-makers are concerned to avoid, preferring to reconstitute the «illusion of reality» that demands that the spectator exercise his «suspension of disbelief». Let me cite Brecht again:

> *The ordinary director, concerned to work as true to nature as possible . . . concerned to*

provide as indistinguishable an imitation of a work of art as possible, attempts to conceal all the failings of his apparatus in giving this true-to-nature reflection. . . . He is miles away from any inkling that precisely these failings of his apparatus might be advantages, for this would imply a refunctionalisation (Umfunktionierung) *of the film.* (Brewster, 1975, pp.20–1)

In this respect Straub/Huillet's use of black spaces in *Introduction* is of particular interest. The immediate observation to be made is that these black spaces break up the film into a series of discrete units. Where they occur during the reading of the letters to Kandinsky, they mark points where something has been omitted from the original letters. The black spaces thus mark the materiality of the text, emphasise its montage construction, foreground the discontinuous structure of the film. The «failings of the apparatus» that would normally be masked through «invisible editing», the imposition of an apparent continuity upon discontinuous materials, is here refused by Straub/Huillet's articulation of the black spaces, which occupy substantial portions of the film's running time.

But even while their initial function may be described in terms of a Brechtian distancing, there is a second function of equal import: they become a crucial affective instrument, a way not of denying emotion, but of infusing it. For example, examine the transition between photographs of the young and old Schoenberg, where the black space works as an extraordinary, rhythmic, mode of punctuation; or the utilisation of the black sequences as key phrases are uttered, as a means of underlining: «no one will be able to read»: «not the case»: «But where should anti-semitism lead, if not to violent deeds? Is it so hard to imagine this?» The sudden blackness in each case crystallises the horror, the urgency, of the verbal text. At another moment the black space is used to *speed* a transition, it become almost a jumpcut, in so far as the voice rushes on: we are aware it is a different take (the tone of the recording is different, deliberately). What must be noted is that the use of black spaces is not constant, in length (they vary between one and nine seconds) or effect. Rather, Straub/Huillet use the black leader as a primary means of articulation, of expression. Every occurrence of black leader is different from all the other occurrences in the film: it is not a mechanistic device, but one that acquires its own aesthetic force, coherence, through the systematicity of its articulation. Speaking of the ten-measure introduction to Schoenberg's early song *Lockung*, Adorno described its organisation into groups, saying that «None of the groups conspicuously repeats anything from the preceding ones, yet all are related through intervening variation.» Straub/Huillet's articulation of the black leader is related to this notion of «developing variations», in so far as repetition is avoided (and through avoiding repetition, the solidification, codification, of meaning is averted). And this avoidance of repetition takes us back to the Brechtian notion of distanciation, since identification, security can only occur when we confront the known, the repeated. Thus the sequence of the second reader in the studio is markedly different, while similar, to the first: there is a new distanciating element in that the camera is now behind a glass window that separates us from the reader, and there is an enigmatic empty screen behind him (just as the next shot, of the coffins, is presented as a frame within a frame of a different kind).

In short, we may say that Straub/Huillet's black spaces constitute exactly the point of intersection of Schoenberg and Brecht in *Introduction*. I began by discussing the nature of *Introduction's* social and cultural intervention; its textual *force* — its ability to *move* audiences — remains, ultimately, unanalysable because as Barthes has pointed out, «pleasure» can be expressed in words, bliss/*jouissance* cannot. *Introduction* is indeed an instance of *jouissance* more than of *plaisir*: it leaves «culture in pieces», it leaves «language in pieces», and yet the loss of that security is not experienced by us as loss, but as the reopening of barred paths, as the reformulation of aesthetic activity.

This article originally appeared as « ‹Introduction to Arnold Schoenberg's Accompaniment for a Cinematographic Scene› : Straub/Huillet: Brecht: Schoenberg» in *Camera Obscura*, No. 2, Fall 1977, and is reproduced here by kind permission with only minor alterations.

«Moses and Aaron»: Straub and Huillet's Schoenberg

[. . .] Schoenberg wrote the three-act libretto, and composed the music for the first two acts, in 1930–32 (just prior to his return to the Jewish faith in 1933); he never completed the music for the third. The story of Moses spreads over the first five books of the Old Testament, but Schoenberg's libretto is principally based on events recounted in Exodus, chapters 3, 4 and 30–32; however, the libretto is not a simple transposition of the biblical account, but reorders and reformulates the biblical sequence.

Schoenberg's libretto commences with «The Calling of Moses» by the voice from the burning bush «free the people». Moses pleads that «my tongue is not flexible. I can think but not speak», and is consequently given Aaron to be his mouth. Thus the fundamental tension between Moses and Aaron is introduced: Moses has the idea, Aaron the ability to transmit it through song. Schoenberg's setting of the vocal parts underlines this relation by having Moses limited to a speaking part, whose rhythm is precisely denoted but whose pitch is only approximately indicated; Aaron's role, on the other hand, is an entirely sung tenor role. The treatment of the chorus (the People) oscillates between these two extremes of sung and spoken parts. After Moses and Aaron have met in the desert, they go to proclaim the message of God to the people, and in order to convince them of God's power, Aaron turns Moses' staff into a snake. He then performs a second miracle, turning Moses' left hand leprous in order to rally the people's courage to fight against their oppressor, Pharaoh. Aaron continues his persuasion of the people by arguing that

This is your own blood, that gives the land nurture, as the flow of the Nile. You fatten the servants of falsehood, the slaves of false gods. But the Almighty One will free you and free your blood . . . He will then lead us to a land where milk and honey flow. *	*It is your blood that nourishes the land, like the water of the Nile. Fat are you making the servants of the lie, of the false Gods. Yet the Almighty frees you and your blood . . . he will lead you into the land where milk and honey flows.*

*This quotation and the ones that follow are from the translation of Schoenberg's libretto which accompanies the Philips 6500 836/7 recording. The Straub/Huillet translation of the original German, referred to below, is given on the right.

and supports his song with another miracle, turning the water in a pitcher into blood and back again to water. This persuades the people «to serve Eternal God» and await being led into the promised land. The Second Act takes place before the Mountain of Revelation; Moses has been gone for forty days and nights, the people become restless at this absence, their faith wavers, and in his fervour to steady them, Aaron conjures up the Golden Calf, around which five butchers dance prior to their slaughter of the animals to be eaten during the orgy. The orgy scenes — of drinking, love-making — occupy much of the second act, climaxing on the people's cry: «Holy is genital power.» Moses descends from the mountain, and banishes the Golden Calf:

> Begone, you image of powerlessness to enclose the boundless in an image finite!

> Begone, thou image of the inability to grasp the boundless in an image.

There follows a long debate between Moses and Aaron, Aaron defending his creation of the Golden Calf, saying

> When you remained apart we believed you were dead. And since the people had long expected both law and commandment soon to issue from your mouth, I was compelled to provide an image for them.

> When thou makest thyself solitary thou are thought dead. The people had waited long upon the word of thy mouth from which rule and law spring. So I had to give it an image to look upon.

Moses, however, insists that the people «must grasp the idea, it lives only for that». This, of course, is the central conflict of the opera, that between the idea and its image, its realisation, as Moses underlines yet again, in the closing words of Act Two:

> Inconceivable God! Inexpressible, many-sided idea, will You let it be so explained? Shall Aaron, my mouth, fashion this image? Then I have fashioned an image too, false, as an image must be. Thus I am defeated!

> Unrepresentable God. Unspeakable, many-meaning idea. Dost thou permit this interpretation? Dare Aaron, my mouth, make this image? Thus have I made myself an image, false, as an image can only be. Thus am I beaten.

The third act is very brief and takes place some time later, consisting merely of an exchange between Moses and a captive Aaron; Aaron defends his action:

I was to speak in images, while you spoke in ideas; I was to speak to the heart, you to the mind.	*In images had I to speak, thou in concepts; to the heart, where thou speakest to the brain.*

and Moses responds by claiming that Aaron

Having been alienated from the source, from the idea, won the people not for the eternal one, but for yourself . . . Here images govern the idea, instead of expressing it.	*From the source, from the idea estranged, didst win the people not for the Eternal, but for thyself . . . Here the images rule over the idea, instead of expressing it.*

Moses' final action is to free Aaron; here Schoenberg's stage directions indicate that Aaron, freed, falls down dead.

The opera was never performed in Schoenberg's lifetime. He died in 1951, and it was only three years later, in 1954, that *Moses and Aaron* was finally premiered, in Hamburg. In 1957 it received its first stage production, in Zurich, which was politely though hardly enthusiastically received. Subsequent performances (though infrequent) have steadily increased the opera's reputation, to the point where Schoenberg's biographer Willi Reich acclaims it as «one of the most important operas of our time» (Reich, 1971, p. 183). On the whole, however, Schoenberg's reworking of the biblical account has never been taken very seriously by critics until now. Hanns Eisler (Schoenberg's pupil and Brecht's collaborator), as Straub has pointed out, found no merit in it, and the recent volume on Schoenberg by Charles Rosen claimes: «The libretto cannot be taken seriously as literature.» (Rosen, 1975, p.94)

Straub/Huillet's reading of it is far more positive, and their orientation may be suggested through a comparison of the English text of the libretto published with the Philips recording of the opera and the translation made by Straub/Huillet. For Straub/Huillet's translation emphasises the libretto's political elements, the power relations between Moses and Aaron, the place of the people with respect to this struggle, and tends to minimise the theological aspects. In the context of the opera's composition between 1930–32, these power relations are of central importance for Schoenberg, engaging with the problematic of leadership: who shall lead the people, and will they be led to the desert, or to the land of milk and honey? Should the people follow the principles embodied in the Tablets of the Law (the Tablets that Moses shatters, despairingly, near the end of Act Two) or those of the Golden Calf? In the context of Hitler's rise to power, the libretto takes on a force very different to its usual interpretations, such as that expressed in the notes to the Philips recording: «The conflict between Moses and Aaron is a universal human conflict between recognition of the supernatural and the role of religion and the ‹Church› in the world.»

Straub/Huillet's production is clearly counterposed to such interpretations (as I shall argue more fully further on), but it is less easy to determine how it relates to Schoenberg's vision of his opera. As I said above, Schoenberg never heard the work performed, and only occasional references to the work are to be found in his published *Letters*. One such, written in 1951, shortly before his death, dwells upon the religious and philosophical significances of the opera (Schoenberg, 1964, no. 244), while a letter dating from 1933 reads:

The elements in this tremendous subject that I myself have placed in the foreground are: the idea of the inconceivable God, of the Chosen People, and of the leader of the people. (op. cit., no. 151)

As always in his life, Schoenberg avoided any *openly* political intent. (op. cit., no. 224) And yet the composition of *Moses and Aaron* was followed shortly after by his dismissal from the Prussian Academy of Fine Arts, his departure from Germany, to Paris, and then his official return to the Jewish faith.* In short, in its social context, *Moses and Aaron* remains a profoundly political statement, «a provocation» as Straub maintains in the interview; and the Nazis themselves were well aware of the political implications of Schoenberg's work (see Appendix). That Schoenberg refused to acknowledge the political implications of his music is not, finally, of any great significance for our present assessment, however.

What does matter is that Straub/Huillet's production of *Moses and Aaron* differs from previous performances of the work, and is centrally concerned with political issues, in a variety of ways. One of these was made explicit in an Edinburgh Film Festival discussion. *Moses and Aaron* is a film about *the people*:

I hope that at the end of the film, not only has Moses destroyed Aaron, Aaron has also destroyed Moses . . . One destroys the other, and they are simply two aspects of the same thing. I hope that what is left is only the people, and that the idea of the film is precisely, not just displaced in relation to Schoenberg, but even opposed to him; the idea that you have to invent a politics which starts from below, and that is is not up to the leader to invent it, but it's up to the people themselves. And while these two have destroyed each other and disappeared, you have to start from scratch. (Straub, 1976, p.95)

---

*Schoenberg's Jewish descent, and reconversion to the Jewish faith in 1933, along with his aesthetic modernism, did not make Germany a congenial place to live in the thirties. He was dismissed from his post as professor at the Prussian Academy of Fine Arts, in Berlin, in 1933 (he had been there since 1924), and he moved, via Spain, to America where he settled in Hollywood, teaching at the University of California.

Brecht's departure from Germany was necessitated by his Marxist beliefs, and he lived successively in Denmark, Finland and then, from 1941–7, in Santa Monica, California. The Nazi authorities deprived Brecht of his German citizenship in 1935.

And «a people always has to be moving, not to settle . . . either materially or ideologically». (Straub/Huillet, 1977) It is here that many critics encounter difficulty with the film: it claims to be about the people, yet it is not a populist film, in so far as the *popular* is precisely what is *ideologically settled*. Straub/Huillet's *Moses and Aaron* is indeed about the people, but this does not mean they patronise their audience. Rather they made a film that challenges the viewer to think, in offering something different to the usual television diet:

> *What interested us was the making of a film which would allow a public which doesn't ever go to an opera, to see an opera.* (Straub, 1976, p.92)

That is to say, not just for a cineaste audience, but for a television audience: German television's third channel financed much of the film, and contributions also came from Italian and French television sources. But making a film for television means, for Straub/Huillet, giving an audience an opportunity to watch something that diverges from the norms of that medium, that demands a very active mental effort. Thus when we speak of *Moses and Aaron* as being «about the people», it must be recognised that the people's actual role in the opera is not large, nor is their visual presence very dominant in the film. On the other hand, the entire theme of the opera revolves around the concept of how an idea may be represented to the people; of what kind of leadership that representation then implies. The struggle for dominance between Moses and Aaron occurs only because of their desire to lead the people: behind every moment of Moses and Aaron's shifting power relations lies the people.

Co-extensive with Moses and Aaron's conflict over how to lead the people, is the problem of how to «represent the unrepresentable»: how to realise an idea in an image, without betraying the idea. In short, they are concerned with the ideology of representation, and the film may be read entirely on this level. On the one hand Moses, who possesses the idea (visited upon him by God), is its essence; on the other is Aaron, who has the ability to represent it in a certain way, to transform it through miracles, into a «realistic» representation. Moses recognises that this inevitably falsifies the original idea, but no solution can be reached between them. Thus at the end of the film, as Straub says, «while these two have destroyed each other and disappeared, you have to start from scratch.» This start is precisely the form of representation offered by Straub/Huillet: one which refuses the idealist dichotomy of Moses and Aaron, of the pure idea versus its transparent representations, and poses in its stead a materialist aesthetic. This is why Straub/Huillet, unlike previous directors of the opera, refuse to opt for either Moses *or* Aaron: that would be to miss the point. Rather, the problem is to find a new path, an alternative route that steers between the mysticism inherent in Moses' idea – essence – and the easy, populist, transparent representations that Aaron chooses.

Straub/Huillet's film is itself an alternative path; it presents the opera in materialist terms, through their elaboration of a Brechtian *mise en scène,* as well as renovating the normative concept of opera. In this latter respect, the most striking departure from usual operatic presentations is the decision to perform the opera in the open air – and yet, simultaneously, in a theatre – an ancient amphitheatre, which has the effect at once of underlining the theatrical aspect of opera, while liberating the cast and their voices from the confining claustrophobia of a conventional theatrical space. And also, of course, the *ruined* qualities of the amphitheatre reverberate ironically upon the notion of classical theatre, while the historical distance between that of Moses, and our own, is economically and persistently affirmed. This «opening up» of the notion of opera is vital to an understanding of Straub/Huillet's activity, in so far as it also illuminates their staging of *Moses and Aaron,* their reformulation, for instance, of many of Schoenberg's stage directions, such as those he gives for the orgy sequences, in which

The slaughterers kill the animals and throw peices of meat to the crowd which fights over them. Some people run around with bloody pieces of meat and consume them raw . . . torches are lit and people run to and fro with them . . . In the background the slaughtering and so forth continues.

Straub has spoken of the significant change being the transformation of Schoenberg's simultaneity into a succession in the film. But an equally important aspect of this shift is its de-emphasising of the purely spectacular elements of Schoenberg's directions: while it is easy to imagine Cecil B. DeMille handling instructions such as those quoted, Straub/Huillet's tactic is one of minimising the voyeuristic potential.

At this point we engage with a characteristic of Straub/Huillet's films, in so far as this avoidance of the spectacular may be most readily described in terms of its relation to the tendencies of the dominant narrative tradition, in which the use of sound, editing, camera-placement, and so on, is directed toward a strengthening of the authority of a film's image-track. The ideology of the visible: seeing is believing. Brecht attacked this conception, when he said that «the simple reproduction of reality tells us nothing at all about that reality»; and Stephen Heath has further suggested that «a materialist practice of film must . . . be inevitably involved in combat against the sublimation of film in the luminous reality-truth of the photograph». Straub/Huillet minimise movement in their films, and thereby, in a sense, begin to question the «reality-truth» of the motion-picture. Thus the first shot of *Moses and Aaron* begins with a high-angle medium close-up of the back of Moses' head: he is singing, but we do not see his face, his mouth. The shot thus leads us to recognise that this is, in the fullest sense of the word, a *sound* film that we will *listen* to as much as look at. And the high angle ensures that the only background to Moses' head is brown earth – no sense of a detailed background, which is quite the opposite of Schoenberg's tendency as evidenced in his stage directions for the orgy scenes. For there the stage was to be filled with a multiplicity of actions and gestures, a plenitude of visual detail which would, Straub/Huillet feel, detract from the force of the music itself. Straub/Huillet's visualisation of the orgy scenes recalls Brecht's provocative but useful conviction that cinema is «by nature static, and must be treated as a succession of *tableaux*». That drunkenness is an aspect of the orgy is shown by a close-up of a pair of hands holding a goatskin of wine, which is poured into a succession of bowls that enter frame left, one by one. The first four are neatly filled, but the fifth is slopped, and the goatskin still pours forth wine after the bowl is full. This simply conceived shot signifies, in the most direct manner, decadence; it is simply a *sign* of drunkenness. The same semiotic simplicity characterises the series of *tableaux* shots that precede the goatskin sequence, as the camera pans through the darkness from one formal vignette (two people in each case — a man showing a boy a knife, two people examining a length of cloth, a tall man pouring wine on the head of a very surprised, shorter man!) to another — always maintaining the camera's *distance* from these scenes and avoiding any sense of «accidentally» catching «life as it happens».*

Another way in which this distanciation is effected is through Straub/Huillet's refusal to situate the viewer *within* the world represented, in contrast to classical narrative procedure. Classical narrative's shot and reverse shot technique gains its psychical efficacy by placing the camera just to one side of the eye-line (the direction of gaze) of each of the characters (e.g. over-the-shoulder shots, or, more commonly, the camera being where the shoulder of the character hypothetically is), so that the spectator is placed in a position effectively *within* the space of the narrative. Direct eye-contact with the camera/spectator is avoided (a «rule» Godard delighted in breaking; and Ozu is another director who, for very different reasons, used to shoot «straight-on» occasionally), but the camera/spectator's angle of orientation is only slightly offset, thereby creating the possibility of the spectator's feeling of inclusion in the scene — in short, establishing the basis for an identificatory situation.

---

*The distance here referred to is both physical and psychical: physical in so far as we are not given a close-shot to clarify, for instance, the precise qualities of the knife, or the textures of the cloth that are being examined — we are given no very detailed or specific information in these shots, and thus remain outside these actions. At which point we are already talking of psychical distancing — the camera's physical detachment, from the events represented, and the formality of the *mise en scène* of this series of *tableaux*, contributes to the psychical distancing of the spectator, that enables him/her to cast a critical eye upon what is being presented on the screen, rather than passively accepting it as a natural «slice of life», presenting «the world as it is». An important aspect of this distance is that it draws attention simultaneously to the signifying activity as well as to what is signified: the *tableau* structure of this sequence avoids any potential «naturalisation» of the image. What is at work here, then, is fundamentally a Brechtian alienation effect, one that in this instance clarifies the social relations not of the figures on the screen, but between those figures and the spectator.

In *Moses and Aaron* — as in most of Straub/Huillet's work — the camera is set at a severe diagonal to the performers, and this diagonal orientation exists not only with respect to the camera's lateral placement, but also to its vertical: a pair of shots of Moses in the first Act, for instance, are medium close-ups in which Moses' gaze passes *beneath* the camera/ourselves, which has a curiously estranging effect. Through strategies such as these Straub/Huillet ensure that no identificatory/illusionist world can be constructed by the viewer, since s/he is systematically denied access to such a world through the refusal of the codified strategies that ensure what is classically known as *continuity*. This quotation from *A Primer for Film-making* is representative:

> *The film-maker must consider the overall action of the scene, and how it can be joined to the next scene, allowing the action to flow smoothly. Without continuity a film would be a series of jumbled images lacking meaning and purpose. As each shot came on the screen, the audience would have to be concerned anew with what the relationship of each image was to the one preceding, and what the particular image meant to the film as a whole. Continuity answers such questions easily and instantly.* (Roberts and Sharples, 1971, p. 145)*

Straub/Huillet refuse to give us such a continuity — but not at the cost of incoherence — neither *Moses and Aaron* nor any of their films is «a series of jumbled images lacking meaning and purpose»: rather, the organisation of their images has a purpose opposed to the «transparency» that the *Primer* sets up as prerequisite. Instead of editing in a manner designed to establish a pyschologically «naturalistic» relation between, say, Moses and Aaron, Straub/Huillet's editing and choice of camera position construct a formal set of relations that both emphasises the materiality of this text and commences to break down the unity and coherence of the space in which the opera's actions take place. Although we are firmly located in an oval amphitheatre, it is sometimes impossible (thanks partly to the high-angled camera that often situates brown earth as the backdrop to the singers), particularly in the opening section of the second Act, to mentally reconstruct the «real» space in which the actions occur. For instance, the sequence of exchanges between Aaron and the male chorus at the beginning of Act 2 is geographically opaque — both are shown looking out left-frame, although narratively they are addressing each other and there is no obvious violation of the 180° rule. The effect of such moments is indeed to force us to ask questions in the manner the *Primer* deems unnecessary. But it is not merely a matter of asking questions: it is one of recognising an alternative mode of cinematic organisation.

Let us examine a few shots from the first Act. Shot 3 is the first time we see Moses and Aaron in frame together, and it is the *only* time we see them facing

---

*I am grateful to Ron Burnett for drawing this to my attention.

each other, Moses on the left, Aaron on the right (Moses is to Aaron's left throughout the film). The cut from shot 3 to shot 4 *seems* to be a continuity cut, since it is to a profile close-up of Aaron, looking out left, as in shot 3. But then shot 5 is a high *frontal* close-up of Moses (whose gaze passes beneath the camera) and shot 6 is another profile close-up of Aaron — except now he is looking out frame right. The camera has moved, with no apparent diegetic motivation, 180° in two 90° jumps. Shot 7 is from the same angle of orientation as shot 5, though from a greater distance. (See Figure 1.)

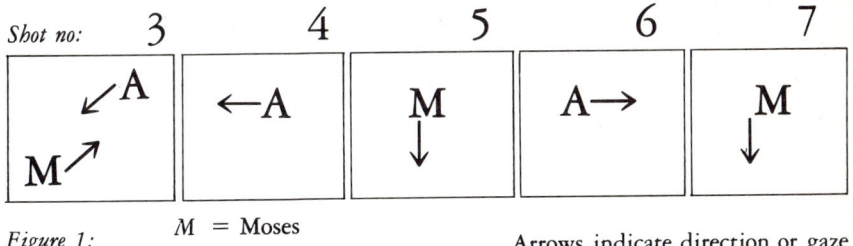

Shot no: 3   4   5   6   7

```
┌─────┐ ┌─────┐ ┌─────┐ ┌─────┐ ┌─────┐
│  ↙A │ │ ←A  │ │  M  │ │ A→  │ │  M  │
│ M↗  │ │     │ │  ↓  │ │     │ │  ↓  │
└─────┘ └─────┘ └─────┘ └─────┘ └─────┘
```

Figure 1:   M = Moses
                 A = Aaron   Arrows indicate direction or gaze

In other words, the coherent theatrical space established quite conventionally in shots 3 and 4 is then dismantled — but dismantled in a manner that emphasises, in fact, the nature of the relationship between Moses and Aaron. In so far as shots 4 and 6 bracket shot 5, Aaron metaphorically surrounds Moses — is his voice; it is difficult to verbalise the effect of this, but the way in which Aaron *surrounds* Moses in these shots has a very bizarre resonance. Formally, however, there is more to be noted, for Straub/Huillet's patterning of these cuts finds its echo in a single shot only moments later. Shot 10 begins in a high long shot of the Priest, then pans left to the people's chorus, then left to the trio of the women, young man and older man, and then back right to the chorus to close the shot on the chorus. The four-element structure (see Figure 2) here is symmetric with the shape of shots 4 to 7: that is to say the fourth element repeats the second (i.e. shots 5 and 7 in the first instance, the two appearances of the chorus in the second instance), and in both cases the second element (Moses/the chorus) is bracketed by a leftward gaze/camera movement, and a rightward gaze/camera movement. Described thus, the sequences sound formalistic in the most sterile manner — but in the film it is not so: for what is going on here (and this is only one example) is something akin to Schoenberg's own notion of «developing variations». Charles Rosen has written of Moses and Aaron that

> *All the music of this immense work is drawn from the transformations of a single series: it is the triumph of Schoenberg's ideal of drawing a wealth of themes from a single source.* (Rosen, op. cit., p.94)

And Straub/Huillet's structuring of their film seems to work in a similar manner: take for instance their handling of the relations between Moses and Aaron, the first few shots of which we examined above. The only repeated element throughout the film is that Moses is always on the left of Aaron: in every other respect, their visual relationship is constantly shifting, never repeated. There is not room here to describe in detail the nature of this shifting, but its parameters are partially defined in terms of the exploration of on-screen/off-screen space, of a camera which moves in mid-shot to eliminate one or other of them (or, reciprocally, to include both of them within a one-shot), in terms of editing mis-matches (i.e. successive shots place Moses and Aaron in identical portions of the frame, suggesting, according to the usual narrative conventions, that they are one and the same person); and so on to the Third Act, in which Moses stands over the bound Aaron, thus posing vertical versus horizontal, cementing visually their irreconcilability, before the camera moves in to definitively separate them, tracking first to Aaron, then panning up to Moses.

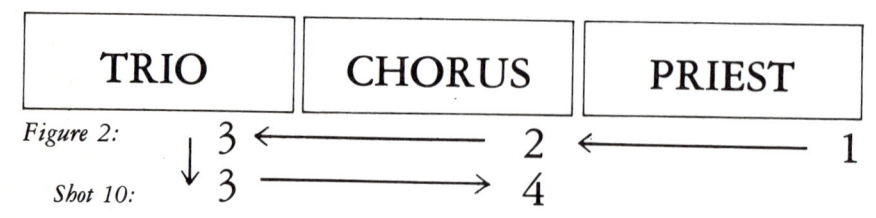

TRIO	CHORUS	PRIEST

Figure 2:   ↓ 3 ←   2 ←   1

Shot 10:   3 →   4

The numbers indicate the successive stages of a camera movement which in actuality is a pan through somewhat less than 180°. The arrows indicate direction of camera movement.

The way in which Straub/Huillet order the film may perhaps be further clarified by reference to Theodor Adorno's description of Schoenberg's early song, «Lockung»:

In its 10-measure introduction three sharply contrasting groups, also distinct in tempo, are juxtaposed; the first consisting of 4 measures, the other 2 of 3 each. None of the groups conspicuously repeats anything from the preceding ones, yet all are inter-related through intervening variations. (Adorno, 1967, pp. 153–4)

It is exactly this lack of repetition that is crucial to comprehending one area of Straub/Huillet's work. For, as the work of Christian Metz and of Raymond Bellour on classic American narrative has shown, repetition is central to the establishment of a «transparent» world on film: shot and reverse shot, eye-line matching, the point-of-view shot are some of the formal structures of codification vital to classical narrative, in so far as identification can only occur when we confront the known, the repeated. An important function of Brechtian distancation is to avoid this «fixing in position», this structural solidification, and it connects interestingly to Schoenberg's work, of which Adorno wrote:

ordering categories, which reduce the difficulties of active listening at the cost of the pure elaboration of the work, are eliminated. (op. cit., p. 153)

When Adorno writes «eliminated», we should not of course think that therefore order is eliminated — for the textual system of the work is itself ordered, though without reference to any external constraint or rule. When the *Primer* speaks of continuity, it is referring to an external set of rules, *according to which* any film must be formed. These are the rules Adorno is referring to when he speaks of the elimination of ordering categories. And *Moses and Aaron* should be approached similarly; just as *History Lessons* is remarkable partly for its work on editing, its magnificently inventive systems of camera placement and editing which «set» each episode of the Brecht text, so *Moses and Aaron* is notable for the variety of its investigations of the concept of «the shot».

In my comments on shot 10 above, evidently one of the things already occurring here, which is different from the general tendency of their previous work (there are exceptions), is camera movement. That is, an important aspect of the filmic work of *Moses and Aaron* occurs within the shot, unlike *History Lessons*, where the focus of attention lies between shots. Again there is no space here to elaborate fully on this aspect of *Moses and Aaron*, but I would like to point to one or two moments of interest. The film's one «production number» (every «musical» has to have one!), the dance before the Golden Calf, is choreographed in a manner finely dislocated from the homogenised synchronicity of a Busby Berkeley routine. Here, at every moment, either one or two of the five dancers is out of synchronisation with the rest — yet always in a rhythmic manner. At some points the dislocation is temporal — two of the dancers' actions occur half a second after the other three, and at other points it is spatial — one dancer being a couple of paces too far to right or left. The resulting effect has a stunning vigour and vitality quite different to our normal experience of dance routines on film. And it is further worth noting that the manner in which the dance ends, with the dancers exiting out of the bottom of the frame, finds its parallel in the scene with the snake, which exits in like manner, each instance being the unorthodox culminating point of a sequence of specifically voyeuristic fascination («It holds us in its spell», cry the people of the snake) in contradistinction to the rest of the film.

Another shot makes an interesting paradox of Bazin's claims for the superior «reality» of a long take, which respects the continuity of both space and time. During Act 2, the people make some offerings to the altar of the Golden Calf, and a final few offer «the final living moments that are still remaining to us . . . » («the last moments that we have to live») at which the camera instantly pans left to frame the male chorus, who say «They have slain themselves as offering!» («They have killed themselves.»). In this shot we do indeed have continuity of space and time, and yet *diegetically* it is discontinuous: the men haven't yet had time to kill themselves! Other camera movements are designed largely as punctuation for the music (the rapid pan to Moses in Act 1 which is promptly truncated by the cut to the next shot, for example), or as languid, almost pantheistic explorations of rocks, bushes and sky through which the music permeates. Or take the notable tracking shot through a semi-circle of Moses and Aaron in the first Act: although the shot may be considered as part of the system of «developing variations» of the sound/image relations between Moses and Aaron, it is also very closely linked to Schoenberg's own stage directions:

> From the audience Moses and Aaron continue to appear [the chorus has previously been singing about these shifting appearances] to exchange their respective positions. At the outset, Moses stands away from him . . . Here Moses begins to retreat, and Aaron appears ever more in the foreground . . . Moses is alone at a considerable distance in the background. Aaron looms large in the foreground . . . Moses ever closer in the foreground, Aaron moves back closer to Moses.

Straub/Huillet's *mise en scène* respects the sense of an oscillating power struggle that is Schoenberg's concern here, but instead of having Moses and Aaron move (they remain static throughout the shot), the camera moves, the relative sizes of Moses and Aaron shifting in the frame as the camera tracks around them and back again. The shot thus functions narratively, but Straub/Huillet simultaneously accomplish more than this, since their materialist use of the medium becomes apparent once again, this time through the contrast between the rapidly shifting background of the amphitheatre, and the slowly changing relations between Moses and Aaron: this dramatic separation of foreground and background has a strong two-dimensionalising effect, similar in some ways to Godard's lateral tracks in *Weekend, La Chinoise,* or *Tout va bien.*

The operatic form is of course by definition suited to the kind of gesticity favoured by Brecht (recall, for instance, his opera, *Rise and Fall of the City Mahagonny*), and Straub/Huillet's direction of the performers' movements is sensitive both to the demands of a Brechtian *mise en scène*, which keeps the arbitrary (as opposed to natural) aspect of those movements in view (i.e. that they are designed to signify, not just to «be»), and to the demands of the music. Thus frequently the most memorable gestic moments occur at the opening or closing of a sung passage: Moses very slowly lowers his hand to his side, as the music equally slowly dies; the young woman who sings shortly afterwards inaugurates her song by lowering her black shawl from her face – uncovering her mouth to make way for the song; or we might note the slump of the invalid woman at the end of her song, or Moses' final fall to the ground at the end of Act 2. It might be objected that such moments are not «social gests» in Brecht's sense («the social gest is the gest relevant to society, the gest that allows conclusions to be drawn about the social circumstances» – Brecht, 1964, pp. 104–5); but they do mark the social relationship that exists between the spectator and what is on the screen, such moments breaking any tendency to accept these images as a transparent «illusion of reality». And also, of course, the gest in each of these cases serves to punctuate the opening or closing of an episode in a decisive manner, as suggested by Brecht: «the individual episodes have to be knotted together in such a way that the knots are easily noticed». (op. cit., p. 201)

Moses and Aaron is full of delightful details, such as occurs during Aaron's miracle of turning water into blood: the camera is in close-up on the pitcher grasped by Aaron's hands, and the blood that was poured from it on to the ground, while we *hear* Aaron singing — and the striking moment comes when he stops singing, and the fragments of his body that are in frame relax, the body tension necessary to singing is released, delicately underlining the relations between on- and off-screen space, between sound and image. The exact effect of such tiny details is difficult to verbalise, but *Moses and Aaron* is full of such pleasures, particularly aural ones: the sound of sheep and cows blending in with Schoenberg's music at one point (recalling Bresson's dictum that «noises must become music»), the sound of blood being poured on the altar, of bowls breaking over the cliffs, and the frequent shots where we watch a frame evacuated of human presence to await the ending of the sound elements before the cut comes. This utter respect for the sound-track (at points we watch a black screen, to focus our listening) has always characterised Straub/Huillet's work, and *Moses and Aaron* is no exception.*

This review began by remarking upon the convergence of Brecht and Schoenberg in Straub/Huillet's recent work, and it is appropriate to close by noting the apparent proximity of these figures' views upon cinema. Brecht, as noted earlier, thought cinema to be «by nature static» and that it should therefore «be presented as a succession of *tableaux*». A critic has spoken of his approach to *The Life of Edward II* as «a fragile structure suspended in unrealistic space», a concept that seems fruitful for the consideration of a Brechtian cinema, in so far as it focuses upon a refunctionalisation of the notion of montage, of editing — such as we find in *Moses and Aaron* in the lack of eye-line matches, of shot and reverse shots, and so forth. Similarly, in 1913, when it was proposed that Schoenberg's *Die glückliche Hand (The Lucky Hand)* might be filmed, Schoenberg was quite emphatic about his orientation toward such a project:

> *My foremost wish is for something the opposite of what the cinema generally aspires to. I want the utmost unreality. The whole thing should have the effect (not of a dream) but of chords. Of music. It must never suggest symbols, or meaning, or thoughts, but simply the play of colours and forms . . . just as music never drags around a meaning with it . . . so too this should simply be like sounds for the eye.*
> (Schoenberg, op. cit., Letter 18)

---

*To get an idea of the complexity of the sound recording (the orchestral track was recorded in a studio in Vienna and the vocal sections were recorded live in the amphitheatre to earphone playback), one should read the dual account of the film's shooting by Gregory Woods and Danièle Huillet which has been published in English in the magazine *Enthusiasm*. Indeed this work journal should be read not merely for its account of the musical recording complexities, but as a document that reveals the importance of *process* for Straub/Huillet.

Straub/Huillet's *Moses and Aaron* manages to fulfil this desire to a considerable degree. But their claims for a specific radical content are in some respects undercut by the formal investigations of language which are aimed at the elimination of «meaning». As Barthes has put it:

To create meaning is very easy, our whole mass culture elaborates meaning all day long; to suspend meaning is already an infinitely more complicated enterprise – it is an «art». (Barthes, 1972, p.272)

Straub/Huillet do, it seems to me, manage to «suspend meaning», but that very suspension eliminates the possibility of any didactic political statement – and this perhaps begins to explain the gap that opens up from time to time between the vision of their films encountered in interviews with them and our actual experience of certain of their films. That this gap exists, however, should not be taken to indicate a fatal flaw, but simply an arena for further thought, discussion, examination. For *Moses and Aaron,* while of considerable significance for radical aesthetics, and political thinking in broader terms, remains a film of uncommon beauty and intelligence, full of «sounds for the eye». Straub/Huillet have not played Aaron to Schoenberg's Moses.

APPENDIX

The Nazis were quick to recognise the political threat of their cultural antagonists, as Brecht, for one, observed after his session with the German censor with respect to cuts in *Kuhle Wampe.** Thus Nazi opposition to Schoenberg's musical practice was immediate, and their analysis in some respects acute, given their interests. The paragraphs that follow here come from a Nazi *Dictionary of Music,* published in the late 30s; they demonstrate quite precisely one perspective from which Schoenberg's work is indeed of revolutionary importance. This idea is argued more fully in the article entitled «*Introduction to Arnold Schoenberg's ‹Accompaniment for a Cinematographic Scene›* : Schoenberg: Brecht: Straub/Huillet» (see p.76).

Schoenberg, Arnold. Vienna 13. IX. 1874, Prof. Comp., 1925/33 Head of a master's class for musical composition at the Prussian Academy of Arts in Berlin.

Schoenberg began his career as composer initially as an epigone of Wagner (string sextet «Verklärte Nacht» (Transfigured Night), «Gurrelieder» (Songs of Gurra etc.), only to depart increasingly in the later course of his development from the traditional principles of all musical forms and creativity, and finally – from his piano pieces op. 11 onwards – consciously dispensed with them completely. «Thereby he upsets», as is stated in the comprehensive publication *Die Juden in Deutschland (The Jews in Germany),* ** «the concepts of consonance and dissonance and thus our entire harmonic

---

*See *Screen,* Vol. 15, No. 2, pp.45–7, Brecht's «A Small Contribution to the Theme of Realism».

***Die Juden in Deutschland,* Institut zum Studium der Judenfrage (6th ed.), Munich 1937 (Eher-Verlag).

system, arrived at through a millenium-long development. In place of our occidental harmony, which is derived from the triad, he later, in a harmonic theory, also seeks theoretically his pettily contrived system of dissonance.» The so-called «twelve-tone music» invented by Schoenberg is also discussed here.

«This twelve-tone music means in music the same thing as Jewish egalitarianism does in all other spheres of life: the 12 tones of the piano should be, under all circumstances, mutually and fully equal, they all must appear in equal frequency, and none is permitted to assume priority over the others. That represents, however, the total overthrow of the natural order of tones in the tonal principle of our classical music.» With these words Karl Blessinger characterises in a brief outline Schoenberg's principle of composition, one which from the Jewish viewpoint was praised as a great revolutionary invention in the area of music.

The biased historical account which was perpetrated by Jewry, especially in the case of Schoenberg, is most clearly shown by drawing a comparison between the edition of the Riemann Music Lexikon which was published by Riemann himself and the 11th edition (1929) which was edited by the Jew Alfred Einstein. Thus, Schoenberg is characterised by Riemann as «a composer who by the extravagances in the invoice of his newest works provokes protest»; his «harmonics» are called «a peculiar hodge-podge of theoretical backwardness and ultramodern negation of all theory». Further, Riemann in particular denounces Schoenberg's tendency to negate everything which has existed up until now – the Jewish tactic of long standing, which was always used when it was necessary to destroy the cultural values of the host-nation and to replace them with their own (which they saw as the only valid ones). Here Riemann writes that «the naïve confession of the author that he has never read any music history gives the key for this unprecedented amateurish concoction» and concluded his reflections with the ascertainment that «the artistic work which Schoenberg pretends to teach, today, thank God, is still strange to the collective sensibility».

With Einstein everything is now reversed. Here Schoenberg appears as «the typical representative or rather exponent of the new music». The Jew Sigmund Pisling similarly wrote that «Schoenberg is by disposition similar to Columbus. He opened a new world of expression for music. Half-repressed melancholy, stammered apprehensions, presentiments which open the eye to the point of bursting, hysterics with which we all live, the multitude of spasms: they become tones.»

The most lapidary formulation of Jewish glorification of Schoenberg was discovered by Paul Bekker: «If on the whole we recognise the possibility of continuity in music as superseding stupid perfection and mechanical operation, then we can only believe this to be possible in the direction of Schoenberg's prophetic art.»

Contrary to this, it must be established that Schoenberg's appointment in Berlin has raised the greatest opposition in non-Jewish circles. In 1925 the renowned musicologist Dr Alfred Heuss (the late publisher of *Zeitschrift für Musik* (Journal of Music) wrote that «the position of Arnold Schoenberg as head of one of the three master's classes for composition at the Prussian Academy of Arts in Berlin signifies a blow against German music which at this time is unsurpassed as a provocation ... The time of Schoenberg's hysterical spasms and shivers in music is now passed ... And now, when German music is just beginning to recover, one dares reward this man's false doctrines with the highest national honours, to emphasise his supposed greatness, showing that one is concerned with neither the development nor the growth of German music. This means a challenge and, if honestly considered, a trial of strength between Germanity and specifically Jewish spiritual conceptions of music.»

Also, it should be noted that Schoenberg, after his emigration from Germany, was soon forgotten – a quick, just sentence of history.

This article originally appeared in *Jump Cut,* Nos. 12/13, 1977, and is reproduced here by kind permission with only minor alterations.

Losey, Brecht and «Galileo»

It is an irony of some magnitude that Ely Landau's American Film Theatre should have chosen to present Bertolt Brecht's *Galileo* as part of its second season. Ironic, at least, for the movie-goer who must pay $4.50 to witness a work by one of the great «left-wing» artists of the century. Brecht's co-optation by the establishment repertoire has been complete for some years now, and this bourgeois recuperation of the radical is neatly underlined by the context of this cinematic version of *Galileo*. Promoted as «high culture» now available to the provincial middle classes, both the advertising and the price-tag are an outrageous confidence-trick designed to appeal to a financial élite (as opposed to the magnificently populist desires of Brecht himself) susceptible to the notion that «*real* art» costs *money*. Just like a «real» theatre, the audience is given an unnecessary interval in the 145-minute film, and even a nice glossy «programme» about the production, replete with witty red cover. On the back page, there's the Biographical Notes — about four inches for director Joseph Losey and star actor Topol, bandying about words such as «famous . . . classics . . . firmest reputation . . . international recognition . . . wide experience . . .» and so on. And there's little more than an inch at the bottom to tell us about Brecht; it lists titles of a few of his other plays; and we read that «He left Germany in 1933 and travelled about Europe until settling in the United States from 1941 to 1947»; then it refers to his «anti-Nazi dramas» and the fact that he «collaborated with Kurt Weill on three musical productions». Sounds like a nice, cheery, humanist kind of fellow, doesn't he?

Curious, though — I mean, weren't Brecht's «travels» necessitated by political persecution? And wasn't that persecution aimed at the most significant political artist to appear since Soviet Russia spawned Meyerhold, Vertov, Eisenstein and the others during the 20s? And didn't the US House Un-American Activities Committee exile him yet again in 1947? Isn't this «programme» a calculated bourgeois revisionism designed to anaesthetise the once radical?

Fortunately, Brecht's *Galileo* rises above the twitching grasp of such whitewashing procedures. One of the strengths of the film, too, is the choice of Joseph Losey to direct it, since back in 1947 Losey had directed its first American performance — the English version which Brecht had meticulously prepared with the equally painstaking Charles Laughton. Indeed it appears that Losey has long harboured a desire to film *Galileo:* «Brecht gave me the exclusive rights to do *Galileo* in English for many years – and I couldn't get anybody to do it . . . I consider the play virtually a scenario for a film . . . the pressure of the Roman Catholic church had barred any possibility of a film in Hollywood, because Laughton and I had tried to do it there before I left.» (Losey, 1967, pp. 168–72) (Losey, like Brecht a few years earlier at the hands of HUAC, was forced by Hollywood's illegal blacklist to leave the USA.) Subsequently, Losey almost raised the money in Europe for a film version, but the offer was withdrawn when Losey felt it beyond his power to *guarantee* the prospective producer «a brilliant performance» (ibid.) Losey's integrity here, his refusal to play the role of either clairvoyant or opportunist, suggests the recuperative *context* of this AFT production may not extend to the film itself.

Nevertheless, when Losey says «my life has been . . . full of *Galileo* since before I ever shot a feature film» (ibid.), we might be curious to know why the anti-illusionist Brecht is so attractive to such a director of the illusionist tradition. In some respects *Galileo* is less «radical» than much of Brecht's earlier work. Formally it is less striking than his work of the 30s, which was more concerned than is *Galileo* with innovations in terms of the mechanics of the performance (interruptive, anti-illusionist devices such as moving platforms on the stage, the use of projected titles, the development of gestic acting, for instance). The emphasis on distanciation, on alienation techniques is not foregrounded in *Galileo* in the manner it is in *The Threepenny Opera,* and Brecht was aware of this: Ernst Shumacher writes that «Brecht regarded *Galileo* as a play with «restricted» alienation effects.» (Shumacher, 1972, p. 214) The reason for this was that Brecht's ideas about drama seemed, in the later years of his life, to shift away from the «epic» theatre, toward a «dialectical theatre». His notions about dialectics were never fully theorised (unlike the notion of epic which was fully outlined in various writings of the late 20s and 30s but *Galileo* seems to embody these ideas in practice. That is to say, the narrative structure of *Galileo* is built in a clearly dialectical manner that is designed to make evident the contradictory forces at work in Galileo's life to pose positive qualities against negative, public images against private, cerebral ideas against physical passions; and these co-existing polarities are organised in a web of complex symmetry. And, as Shumacher has pointed out, this symmetry was clearly worked out by Brecht's preliminary notes for the play. The point of mentioning this is to underline the fact that *Galileo* is not a product of the Brecht valued, say, by Godard and Gorin (whose allegiance centres around the «Notes to the Opera *Aufstieg und Fall der Stadt Mahagonny*» of 1930). For the emphasis on symmetry suggests closure, a concern with «wholeness» and «unity» that is somewhat at odds with the more open-ended theatrical forms of his earlier years, while comparatively consonant with the «illusionist» narrative tradition represented by Losey.

However, in the circumstances, the comparative conservatism of *Galileo* is its virtue: Brecht's concentration on the internal relations of the text (as opposed to its physical relationship to the audience) gives it a coherence and strength that almost *defies* distortion by unsympathetic direction. (Not that Losey is unsympathetic, however.) The play revolves around the figure of Galileo, over the span of his mature life, and this life is related to a crucial moment in intellectual history: the supersession of the Ptolemaic world view (earth as centre of the universe) by the Copernican (sun as centre, earth as planet). Galileo fights for the recognition and acceptance of this new knowledge – for a revolution in consciousness; the play's narrative traces the

contours of this struggle, thereby identifying the strengths and limitations of Galileo's revolutionary endeavour. Brecht presents Galileo's arguments with the ruling nobility of Italy, his clashes with the Church and the Inquisition – in short his struggle to continue his research in pursuit of the truth. The path Galileo took is one presented by Brecht in various lights, both negative and positive: his obsequious courting of favours from the Grand Duke, his readiness to wreck his daughter's happiness in order to continue his research, his recantation of Copernican theory (for fear of physical torture) are set against his ideological veracity, his conviction that «My intention is not to prove that I was right, but to find out *whether* I was right», his brilliant argumentative powers. Brecht's presentation of Galileo is in no sense an idealist one: it presents the man in all his frailties, as both hero (intellectually) and coward (physically), as loving and betraying truth. One fulcrum the play rests on is the scene of Galileo's recantation, which suggests that (idealistically) Galileo betrays truth by recanting, while (pragmatically) he preserves it in preserving his life to enable him to continue his research in secret, for the benefit of later ages.

The dawning of a new age, the inevitable setbacks to its immediate implementation, the difficulties confronting any one individual who sets his sights on such a revolutionary endeavour, these are the concerns of *Galileo*, for we know today how close to impossible it is for any individual to dissociate him/herself from the mechanisms of the dominant society. «By setting the name Medici in the skies I am bestowing immortality on the stars»: Galileo's servility toward the Prince is undoubtedly ironic, since in the scene preceding its utterance, it has been pointed out that Copernican theory effectively abolishes heaven. However ironic Galileo's stance, the fact remains that he is economically dependent on the very culture whose demise his theories announce; clearly there is no ready answer to this dilemma, even today, as Jon Jost's *Speaking Directly: Some American Notes* makes clear. In Jost's case, his retreat to the woods, his attempted withdrawal from intercourse with the dominant ideology has proven elusive: he still needs a camera (product of alienated French workers), and a laboratory to process the film (oppressed technicians?); he still has to take his film from city to city, by automobile. In short, contradiction is inherent in the revolutionary's activity, and might be said to be the essential theme of *Galileo*. Certainly it was a theme that preoccupied Brecht through the 40s, as we see in his analysis of Breughel's pictorial contrasts: «In *The Fall of Icarus* the catastrope breaks into the idyll in such a way that it is clearly set apart from it and valuable insights into the idyll can be gained. He doesn't allow the catastrophe to alter the idyll; the latter rather remains unaltered and survives undestroyed, merely disturbed.» (Brecht, 1964a, p. 157) Similarly Brecht shows that the Copernican «catastrophe» didn't result in any immediate radical transformation of the social order – mass action is the only precedent for that; so the problem remains of how to communicate new and «subversive» knowledge to the masses. *That* dilemma, however, is not the subject of *Galileo* – it is better, therefore, that I return to our immediate task: appraisal of Losey's version of *Galileo*.

As indicated earlier, Losey had wanted to film *Galileo* since the late 40s, so it is not surprising that for the most part (with the exception of the unnecessary music added to Hanns Eisler's original score) he seems to stay close to Brecht/Laughton's original English version. Losey's use of colour, as far as the costumes are concerned, fulfils Brecht's intentions. This is Brecht's own description:

> *Each scene had to have its basic tone . . . the entire sequence had to have its development in terms of colour. In the first scene a deep and distinguished blue made its entrance with Ludovico Marsili, and this deep blue remained, set apart, in the*

second scene with the upper bourgeoisie in their grey-green coats made of felt and leather. Galileo's social ascent could be followed by means of colour. The silver and pearl-grey of the fourth (court-)scene led into a nocturne in brown and black (where Galileo is jeered at by the monks of the Collegium Romanum), then on to the eighth, the cardinal's ball, with delicate and fantastic individual masks (ladies and gentlemen) moving among the cardinals' crimson figures. That was a burst of colour, but it still had to be fully unleashed, and this occurred in the ninth scene, the carnival. Then came the descent into dull and sombre colours. (ibid., p. 167)

In other words, Brecht uses colour and texture of cloth as an index of wealth and power – Marsili's deep blue is of greater opulence than the grey-green of the upper bourgeoisie, and he remains distinguished from them, while the crimson worn by the cardinals serves to designate their omnipotence. At the moment at which Galileo seems to find himself and his theories accepted, he is shown mingling with the crimson-clad cardinals – subsequently as he falls from favour, the vigour of this red disappears from Galileo's environment. Losey remains faithful to this structure, the cardinals' crimson, Ludovico's blue, and the carnival-singer's multicoloured patchwork garb being the only chromatic eruptions to disturb the predominant grey, black, brown and off-white of Galileo's world. Losey ignores any temptation to embellish or decorate Brecht's structure. His work as director is characterised by its restraint; naturally he weights a particular interpretation of the play through his choice of framing, of cuts, and so on, but one does feel his sensitivity to the demands of the text, a stylistic subordination to Brecht's structure: in the scene at the cardinal's ball between Galileo and Cardinal Barberini (who is later to be Pope), the two men exchange a series of epigrammatic proverbs, a verbal duel that builds with intensity to Barberini's climactic and threatening, «Can one walk on hot coals, and his feet not be burned?» Losey's *mise en scène* is elegantly executed, the camera tracking and panning skilfully to relate the two men (the cardinal in red, Galileo in black robes) weaving in and around the white marble pillars that serve to support visually their verbal thrust and parry. Or again, look at the scene of Galileo's recantation, in which we see not Galileo's agony but that of his pupils, contrasted with his daughter Virginia's prayers that he will be «saved». This is one of the dramatic peaks of the play, and Losey reserves for it an expressionistic treatment reminiscent of *Ivan the Terrible* – huge shadows cast on the walls behind the actors, a starkly simple set consisting of a table and chess set on the left (chess the symbol of conflict, that is crucial to this dialectical drama), Galileo's empty chair in the centre, and a skeletal flight of stairs on the right, atop which Virginia prays while Galileo's disciples hover uneasily on the left. Losey allows this tension to develop on the screen by keeping both parties simultaneously in the frame, with only minimal use of close shots. The clarity and power of this scene is quite extraordinary, the more so by contrast to Losey's restraint elsewhere in the film, which has a rather more naturalistic base.

Not that Losey isn't prey to a certain dogmatism at points – the huge close-up as Galileo speaks directly at the camera, early in the film, prophesying the future significance of astronomy, is one example, but even here one feels Losey's intent is fidelity to the spirit of Brecht's *educative* endeavour (immediately apparent in the very first scene, as Galileo meticulously explains the Ptolemaic world-view to the young Andrea, which he follows with a practical demonstration of the Copernican alternative): for the *surprise* of this large close shot functions to undercut any simple «identification» with the figure of Galileo. Brecht's drama is, of course, an anti-illusionist, anti-identificatory one which demands that we exercise our intellects rather than simply our emotions. In this respect it is salutary to recall Brecht on the actor's responsibility: «At no moment must he go so far as to be wholly transformed into the character played . . . This principle – that the actor appears on the stage in a double role, as Laughton and as Galileo – comes to mean simply that the tangible, matter-of-fact process is no longer hidden behind a vest; that Laughton is actually there, standing on the stage and showing us what he imagines Galileo to have been.» (Brecht, 1964a, pp. 193–4) This is where the film's Brechtianism begins to break down – Topol is not Laughton, and his conception of the role is a simple *immersion* in his notion of «the character» of Galileo; his performance is naturalistic, rather than alienated. This stylistic tension reappears in the film itself: on the one hand, we have the predominantly naturalistic performances of Mary Larkin as

Galileo's daughter, Virginia, and Richard O'Callaghan as Fulgenzio; and on the other, the magnificently Brechtian engagement of Colin Blakely with his role as Priuli, where his gestic vitality imparts an exemplary clarity to his performance — watch the way his hands are used to denote «manipulative thought at work», for instance: it is a didactic performance, but splendidly witty and energetic. Or again, John Gielgud's cameo scene as the expostulating and aged cardinal is a caricature of exquisite balance, culminating in his physical collapse even as he hits the word «immortal». Similarly, the performance of the ballad singer and his wife (Clive Revill and Georgia Brown) has a direct vigour that recalls much of the spirit of Lotte Lenya and the visual power of Breughel.

And yet — well, the essential problem with the film as far as Brechtianism is concerned lies in Losey's very fidelity to the «distanciation» techniques of the original production: in the intervening twenty-eight years audiences have become so used to such devices that they no longer function efficaciously. Brecht's episodic structures — for instance the use of the chorus and printed titles — no longer alienate us in the manner they once did. The point behind «distanciation» is that we are provoked into thought, jolted into exercising our rational faculties, rather than allowed to serenely and passively emote throughout the performance. At one time, the use of projected titles on the stage had an interruptive effect, since it cut across the expected conventions of the genre, thereby creating a meaning that could not be *un*-consciously responded to, consumed by the audience. One of the most vital precepts of Brechtian theory is the notion that alienation devices must never be reduced to *mere technique,* or *convention,* for then they become «invisible» and our identificatory propulsions are *not* efficiently interrupted. Thus Losey's Galileo seems from time to time to approach (though not to rival) the spurious «Brechtianism» of Lindsay Anderson's *O Lucky Man*. What Brecht taught, and Godard learned, was that alienation devices must be continually re-invented, if they are to retain any value: thus Godard's distanciation techniques are rarely iterative, but always search for a new mode of expression, in a perpetually heuristic endeavour: one obvious example from the work of Godard/Gorin is their evolving use of the lateral tracking shot, which refuses to allow us to «enter» the «depth» of the frame in the conventional illusionist manner. Another example is constituted by the various disjunctions between image-track and sound-track that recur through Godard's work, from *Bande à part* to *Tout va bien*. What we must note is that the recurrence of this disjunction is in no sense formulaic, but consistently inventive, probing, seeking to surprise and jolt our intellects.

Early in the film Galileo ruminates on the fact that people began to make progress only when ships left the safety of the shoreline — this is the kind of courage Losey lacks; one suspects that the passing of twenty-five years has made little change in Losey's vision of how *Galileo* should be done. And yet, having said this, I feel remorseful – if we stop to think of what the AFT *could* have done to *Galileo,* we should perhaps be thankful for a production of as much integrity as Losey's. Losey may not be the radical director Brecht deserves, but his production is consistently restrained and allows the incomparable intelligence of Brecht's text to thrust through to us. For *Galileo* is one of the very greatest dramas of this century, and it seems to have the rare ability of transcending even the worst production; its verbal profundity, like Shakespeare's, is somehow indestructible, and its articulation of the basic dilemmas of revolutionary consciousness is absolutely haunting. After Galileo's recantation, his pupil Andrea laments «Pity the country that has no hero», to which comes the sombre retort: «Pity the country that *needs* a hero.» This contradiction hangs in the air long after its utterance, resisting dissolution: for as well as the need for mass action (as Galileo suggests), there remains the need which Andrea urges – for the lone bearers of the knowledge that subverts our conventional orientation, that alone may change our consciousness. For it is this knowledge, in the broadest sense, that must lay the base for mass action. To the rarity of this fusion both history and *Galileo* attest.

This article originally appeared in *Jump Cut,* No. 7, 1975, and is reproduced here by kind permission with only minor alterations.

Godard and Me: Jean-Pierre Gorin Talks

Introduction
I've entitled what follows «Jean-Pierre Gorin Talks» in order to make clear that it isn't strictly an interview, although I've constructed the text that follows as one. But that construction came about long after the event itself, and its shape, substance and sequence is principally the result of my reading of sixty pages of tape transcript, a condensation, a collage of that raw material.

The occasion was this: in November 1974 Gorin came to Canada for a two-week trip through various universities. And the trip commenced here, in London (Ontario), at the University of Western Ontario; it was the first time Gorin had made a public appearance since he and Godard first toured with *Tout va bien* in 1972. And it was the first time he had seen the film since then.

I have had a passionate interest in Godard's and Godard/Gorin's work since the mid-60s, and I spent most of my spare time in the couple of weeks preceding Gorin's arrival preparing myself for a taut, testing interview with a political intellectual. But as soon as I met him off the train, it was clear that many changes had occurred: gone was the hard rhetoric, the specifically political orientation (the politics are still there, but subterranean). The next twenty-four hours was a welter of words, on almost every subject. We sat up half the night talking of the Canadian north, Jean-Pierre impulsively deciding to make a film there. We listened to much music — rock, jazz, and African ethnic — and discussed poster art, cooking, the Sahara, Mexico — so much outside the narrow realm I had prepared myself for. So the prepared interview never happened. Much of what I had prepared was clearly irrelevant to the Gorin that confronted me — as his immediate dismissal of *Tout va bien*'s Brechtianism makes clear. His passage through the past two years has been a varied one, culminating in several months with a group of Mexican anthropologists researching witchcraft in the Mexican bushlands.

Indeed the notion of witchcraft absorbs much of his thinking now — he speaks of himself as Godard's apprentice, of himself as somehow taking over from Godard, rather than just learning from him. Whether this is the case, of course, only time will tell. But if energy is anything to go by, Gorin may yet produce work to astound us — if he can raise the money to do so.* In any event,

---
*Since this interview, Gorin has made *Poto and Cabengo*, a feature-length documentary film about twin sisters who had supposedly developed their own language. He now teaches at the University of California, San Diego.

his presence here was completely absorbing; his openness, friendliness — his charm, ultimately — won all who heard him, though I'm aware now of certain inconsistencies in what he said, of points at which his ego won out over modesty. The student paper, in the following week, symptomatically headlined its coverage of his visit «The Bob Dylan of Film?»

Anyway — my planned interview didn't take place. What did happen was this. We screened *Tout va bien*, to maybe 150 people (a good crowd for UWO), then Gorin talked, answered questions for about an hour. The following morning he talked for two hours to a class of about 45 students — very informal, easy, relaxed. So this three hours of talk, when transcribed, came out to about sixty pages — repetitive in places, often talking about one idea at several points, expanding, recapitulating, and so on. What I have done, essentially, is offer *my* reading of what he said. I have, obviously, omitted much; I have trimmed, I have drawn several separate statements together as if they were one, I have invented some of the questions (partly because many of the questions were not audible on the tapes). But I believe this is an accurate and economical representation of what was said by this extraordinary man whose capacity for change surprised us all, a change encapsulated perhaps in these words, offered after the screening of *Tout va bien*:

> I'm a Nietzschean-Marxist. That's all I am. And I'm certainly more Nietzschean than Marxist.

Q. When you and Jean-Luc Godard first toured with *Tout va bien* in 1972 you were making claims for the film that located it very firmly within a Brechtian tradition of political aesthetics; you spoke of it as commencing a period of «materialist fiction», as marking a new beginning for a certain kind of cinema. Do you still see it the same way now?

J-P.G. I like the humour in it. I was amazed because I was less bored than the last time I saw it. Now it seems to me to be a film *about* boredom, rather than a boring film about politics. There is one approach in that film that I'm not going to deal with anymore: I'm no longer a Brechtian. The very idea of trying to think through the lenses of a guy who was thinking in the 30s seems to me, now, extraordinarily backward; what kind of madness tries to delay time and space and history? I'm hardly even a Marxist any more, so it opens my sights a little.

Q. You mean, therefore, it opens the way you see the film tonight; in what way is it different from seeing it two years ago?

J-P. G.   Two years ago it was like putting the mirror in front of the reality and being disturbed because people wouldn't accept that kind of reflection or wouldn't be able to deal with it. *Tout va bien* was quoted by one of the top Gaullists in a television show just before the elections, as demonstrating what some mad leftists could do and want to do to this beautiful country. It was kind of frightening in a way. If I think of the four or five years I spent with Jean-Luc, there is obviously a failure in that we really wanted first to do films — the two of us together — and then to do cheap films and to do films which would, when you see them, give you an idea that you could do the same thing with the same principles and adapt them to your own situation. If you show a film which is done with only stationary and tracking shots, or if you do a film like *Letter to Jane,* you're saying to people: «Use three stills and make a film.» You don't need to enter into the spirit of Hollywood to do it; you can do a $2 film if you want to. The only thing you have to know is that it will be a $2 film in terms of aesthetics. With $2 you can just put the camera this way and that's all. But basically people haven't understood that at all, and constantly we've been labelled as authors with a very élitist practice.

Tout va bien is a very minimal film. It works on two camera moves — the lateral tracking shot and the stationary shot. The people who have a super-eight camera shoot their granny's dinner or baby's breakfast, and they all use the same type of approach, which is the stationary shot. Around 1969 we decided to work this way, which is to say that Jean-Luc, me, Straub etc. are not the people who make a fortune. *Tout va bien* was like making a home-movie in 35mm, worth a quarter of a million dollars, which was rather preposterous. We were also very interested in verbal language: all the talking you keep hearing on the soundtrack is quotation. It's like huge segments of quoted phrases in which our lives are trapped and to which we submit constantly. We don't even take the time to listen to them, or the processing is engineered in such a way that we can't truly listen to them. What *we* were trying to do was repeat those things together and create certain spaces in which people would have the possibility to reflect. And it's a film which tries to make people aware that they are in a movie theatre, with their ass on such and such a piece of material and looking at the movie they have paid for. You are exchanging one dollar or two dollars for a quarter million dollar dream, which is the basic trick in movies.

Q.   Do you feel dissatisfied with what you did during '68 — this occurred to me during Yves Montand's monologue about the nature and limitations of his involvement with the May events.

J-P.G.   No, there's no question of being satisfied or dissatisfied. I think that speech of Montand's was really a joke. I wrote it because I wanted people to be trapped in it, which happened in France. Everyone said that Jean-Luc had written it and that made Jean-Luc furious: it's not him at all. So you get more or less trapped in the monologue by the fact that it's spoken by Montand, it may be Godard, you assume it might be you, and it shifts between three poles all the time. But the most personal thing in terms of things said is Jane's monologue, which was mainly my experience when I was working for *Le Monde* and getting sick to my stomach at being obliged to write in a certain form and not finding any way to fight it, other than being lazy — that kind of despondency you have when you can't find your own wave of expression. This whole film is about that. It's about the people who can't find it.

Q.   In what ways did you and Jean-Luc find your «own wave of expression» in *Tout va bien?* Most critics seized on the film's political dimensions, but few seem to have discussed its visual brilliance.

J-P.G.   Every shot of this film was totally drawn beforehand. I mean, we really knew exactly where the camera was going to be. We really thought in terms of shapes and surfaces and relationships between shapes and surfaces. It's a very composed movie, almost like stills. We did a lot of work on the colours, on the lighting, on getting back to a very classical type of lighting — those images totally in focus at every point which we don't see any more because people zoom around with their camera, so you get that kind of flatness and heaviness of the whole frame. Also the acting: I mean, if you take the workers — all those guys are rediscovering ways to act which were current in France in the 30s. There's a guy acting like Jean Gabin and a girl acting like Arletty, and another guy who acts as if in a film by Vigo, and all that creates an ethical position between their type of acting and the type of acting that Jane and Yves both do. And of course film is a relationship between sound and image; and we were working on that dialectic and tackling the problem the other way around from the way most people do. Most people put an order of value on it: «Film is image.» We said: we don't know if film is image or not, and we're going to start by saying film is just as much image as it is sound and to do that and to make it perceptible we are going to start from the soundtrack, we are going to overcrowd the soundtrack and we're going to skip the image. So the soundtrack of *Tout va bien* is very complex, but on a 16mm print it becomes blurred. You don't perceive the film exactly as it was done. And that's a big problem. Technically, it is sound which has advanced most in the last twenty years. You have this fantastic Nagra to tape sound. But when you go from magnetic to optical you lose a lot because the device is totally archaic. You lose fifty per cent of the sound. So in a sense sound film does not exist – the complexity of the soundtrack, the different levels of the soundtrack, the way music can enter words, and words and noises can melt together, all that is lost. The thing we intended to prove, and it's not proven by this film, is that the politics may be a short trip to poetics which people are not ready to accept.

Q. How did you find working with Fonda and Montand?

J-P.G. It was a fun film to make because we were dealing with big stars. I mean, it was the first time I had approached a big star like Yves Montand or Jane Fonda. And the thing was that obviously in the film they were *not* the stars. The stars were the twenty extras who were paid twenty bucks to play the workers and who really enjoyed themselves a lot. There is a lot of material that we haven't put in the film where they were doing absolutely incredible things, totally incredible things. And we were trapped by our determination to do stationary shots because the most incredible things were happening on the right side and the left side of the camera. At one point, I mean, neither Jane nor Yves knew what they were doing in that film. It was a heavy problem for them to be doing the whole factory sequence, because they're not the centre of attention. I mean, they're on the doorstep and that's forty minutes of this film. So that was very difficult to deal with.

Q. Was the supermarket sequence inspired by the ending of Tashlin's *The Disorderly Orderly?* That was also in a supermarket, and Jerry Lewis just destroyed it.

J-P.G. Well, I didn't consciously make that precise connection; the supermarket scene is a travelling shot, and is a pure homage to Jean-Luc by me, and it's not as good as many of his travellings, but it's not too bad. That travelling was done right on the spot. I'd cancelled the scene twice. First we had to lie to the guys; we told them, «Well, we're making some kind of Jerry Lewis movie. People are going to have a quarrel in the supermarket.» And they said, «Well, that's great. Let's do that.» So there we were in the supermarket – and no ideas, nothing. That huge space, two square miles of goods and 1,000 people. Basically body builders. We had grabbed a whole staff of black body builders. And big guys like that. All around us saying, «What are you going to do?» And finally, wandering in that supermarket with Jean-Luc, we saw that long line of cashiers and we had no rails to do the tracking shot so we just improvised it. Right there. In three hours. And pushing the camera. That was really tough work. And it could have been better if we had two thousand people, the whole scene would have been a riot. But the scene was very funny to deal with because the guys playing the leftists were friends of ours. They were having a ball. And the guys playing the cops were extras paid 20 bucks a day. They were really not having a ball, I know. At one point a guy came to me – an old guy, and he was 65 or 70, I don't know – but he really looked worn out. And he had a big bruise on his helmet, and said, «For 20 bucks I can't accept being hit by pineapple cans. Please tell them not to throw them.» And it was a total riot. And the girls at the cash desks were absolutely amazed to see these punks rioting all over, because that was their job everyday.

Q. I don't know the technical aspects but what happens to the colour in that sequence? It has a very strange quality. Is it filters or . . .

J-P.G. No, there is a trick in the film which you don't see at all on the 16mm print. The film goes gradually from a super traditionally lit set, to *vérité* shooting without banks of special lights. I mean the lighting at the beginning of the film is an approximation of the lighting used in the films of the late 30s and 40s. The most crucial and «realistic» issues are reached in the beginning — the whole strike context. O.K., at that point we use theatre, we use distanciation and we use that cut open factory with the tracking shots and all that. And the film slowly goes into reality and back to no lighting at all. So the sequence in the supermarket is not lit by anything. It's just the neon light. And the neon light gives that type of aquarium kind of light. Like seeing fishes. And of course the last tracking shot sums up the whole film — the slum landscape with that incredible song. You pass along the wall, and on the soundtrack you have the three principal sounds of the film — the leftist sound, the Communist Party sound, the boss sound. They're like sound vignettes stamped on that bare wall. And then you get back into landscape again. That's the summary of the film. It's a film done on a number of sounds and the way they interact with each other.

Q. In all of Jean-Luc's films there are restatements and modifications of scenes from his earlier films. And it seems to me that in *Tout va bien* I want to make all kinds of connections to *Weekend*, to *Pierrot le fou*, to *La Chinoise*, to *Deux ou trois choses que je sais d'elle*. For instance Fonda and Montand's roles here are in one sense a reprise of Seberg and Belmondo's in *A bout de souffle*, it's a kind of rebirth of that. And the opening of *Tout va bien* is a negation or a reworking of the opening of *Le Mépris*.

J-P.G. Yes, that's true. The opening of *Le Mépris* was something forced on Jean-Luc. The producers saw *Le Mépris* and said, «Well, you haven't got enough ass in it.» So Jean-Luc said: «O.K. You want ass in it. You're going to get it.» And he made that sequence where she's lying on the bed and she's saying, «Do you love my ass? Do you love my mouth? Do you love my etc.?» So we did it with two fully clothed people and played on the kind of phoney voice to depict love that stars can use. And she goes into: «I love your balls and I love your knees and I love your big hairy feet.» And it gets totally crazy. It's total parody. To a point where it becomes a little freaky, to be so «Godardian» about everything — you no longer know how to take it.

Q. Do you think this uncertainty, or ambiguity, has anything to do with the nature of your unique directorial collaboration with Jean-Luc?

J-P.G. Yes — maybe the only *new* thing I had was that I didn't want to work alone. I wanted to work with someone. I had no commitment whatsoever to the mystique of the author and I don't think anyone who's serious for one second in terms of film-making — who has to deal with money people, who has to deal with a crew of twenty people – can think about his loneliness as a creator like, you know, a painter or a writer: it's a very collective process. And the thing I wanted was precisely to try to smash that unbelievable image and try to build something new – making films which would have less equilibrium. When you're alone, you can disguise yourself, you can mask yourself, veil yourself. You use various ways to trick people into doing the things you want to do. It's not so easy with two directors. When people saw us on the set of *Tout va bien* getting into an incredible theoretical discussion which, beside the theory, was something very personal because we had done something to each other which we couldn't handle, they had the feeling that the film was falling apart just because there was a more lively process of discussion. And the balance is very difficult to keep because if you go too much into that discussion, at one point the film totally gets out of hand and you can't finish it.

Q. Why are you no longer working with Jean-Luc?

J-P.G. With Jean-Luc and me, it was a love story; we really were deeply in love with each other, with no shame, no guilt; it was a very deep involved sexual thing; we played on our fears and neuroses, it was something which went far beyond movies, and that's why it was effective. What happened is that we really worked together for five years, thirteen hours a day, which is absolutely enormous. You don't get together saying, «Look, ah, we're going to do that masterpiece together», but rather, you get into a process which is absolutely, totally, out of control. But when you work in those conditions there comes a point where you're strangling yourself, you just want to breathe and take some air. So Jean-Luc is more and more into very theoretical, rhetorical film, and working in video.

He's trying to achieve what he's been trying to achieve all his life, which is to be able to do diaries. All Jean-Luc's films are done for a particular ten minutes in them (like *Weekend,* which was made for the long traffic jam sequence) and he's obliged to fill up the middle with something else just to get the normal release length, which is one hour and a half. And now he's going to be able to make those ten-minute films and link them together. He's more interested in that than anything else.

And I started shooting a film which was stopped right in the middle because the main actress was busted for dope dealing. The film I started was a very personal film. It was like curing myself. I wrote a script and nobody could play it. And actors — a lot of interesting actors and good actors — liked the film a lot but they were afraid. It was a film on schizophrenia and was, in fact, a very schizophrenic film in its moods. And people were scared. It was a ritualistic film — almost no dialogue — with situations set in such a way that people would be obliged to act out things. I mean, they would be acted out by the situation. Those situations were really incredibly violent — not physical violence — but in terms of a psychological violence. So finally, not being able to find any actor, I decided to play it myself which was the last thing to do. But that was part of the project. So I played the film myself and totally blew my mind. And it was really strange because when you are both behind and in front of the camera, I mean, you're in the middle. And it's interesting because the people I was working with were people I'd been working with for four years; the same cameramen shot *Tout va bien* and the same crew. And we had a very intense relationship for four months. It was like a free clinic — everybody pulling out a lot of hidden stuff. So the girl freaked out, decided to deal dope, got busted, and the film is unfinished. So from that I went out (which was also a part of the film in a certain way), I went out to wander around Mexico and Guatemala. I wrote a lot of things, shot a lot of stuff and made a lot of sounds and things like that. I came back with the idea that I was going to enjoy myself making movies. I just wanted to play, you know.

Q.   What happened to Jean-Luc's project of making that huge film on France which was going to run for 10 hours or 3 days or something?

J-P.G.   Sometimes we wrote treatments – ten pages of total bullshit, just having fun writing ten pages together just to raise money and being absolutely sure that we'd never make the film, that we'd have the money and that we could go to the beach with it, buy equipment and do a small film. And *Communications** was that kind of project. The fact that it was supposed to be a 24-hour film done by twenty people was to make the dish look more brilliant, but finally nothing really came out of it. That's also the time in Jean-Luc's life when he started at least three projects which never came through (that's before we started working as the Dziga Vertov group) – *Communications*, he started a film in Cuba, and he made a film in the States called *One American Movie*, which was shot by Leacock and Pennebaker, and was such a piece of shit we finally decided not to finish it. And Pennebaker made a version of it (*One P.M.*). It was a piece of shit in the sense that the relationship between Jean-Luc and Pennebaker was absolutely non-existent, Leacock and Pennebaker just did *their* thing zooming and running around, and Jean-Luc just wanted stationary shots. And it's very strange when you see *One P.M.*, because you see Jean-Luc as a zombie in one corner of the screen, being totally unable to grasp those mad monkeys. So the film failed.

Q.   What about the films which followed?

J-P.G.   There was a lot of commitment behind the films we did between 1969 and 1972, a refusal to do classical psychological narrative, and that caused problems. The nine films which we made were mainly sponsored by television, «carte-blanche» given to Jean-Luc and me to do whatever we wanted; that was the case with British TV with German TV. And they all refused to show the films; they banned the films, but not on overt political grounds. Rather, the politics was in another cake. And the cake was: «This is not cinema. You don't know what a film is; you don't know what film is about; you don't know how to take pictures from the beginning with that beautiful fiction that's like the bible»; and in the end you admit that. And all I can say is that a political film is a film which disconnects the normal links of

---

*It is unclear whether or not this project is the same as *Sur et sous la communication (Six fois deux)*: 1976, six television programmes of two fifty-minute sections each, made with Anne-Marie Miéville and available from the BFI Distribution Library.

reality, which suddenly breaks the world apart and gives you space, where suddenly you can think and breathe and deal with the element. And the television bosses just weren't ready for that.

Q. *Tout va bien* is explicitly by Jean-Luc and yourself, where the earlier films were credited to the group. Did the larger collective notion not work as you'd hoped?

J-P.G. Well, take *Vent d'est*, which was a post-'68 project. Daniel Cohn-Bendit, called Danny the Red, was heavily into Westerns, like the Sergio Leone type of thing. He wanted to do a Western so he wrote a vague treatment and the money was raised purely on the media star basis of Jean-Luc, Danny the Red, and Gian Maria Volonté — names being put together that might make a film. So we got 19 million liras to do the film and we did it for 10 million and gave away 8 million to political groups and people who were doing interesting things like that. It turned out that all those political groups were mainly managed by crooks who bought themselves famous paintings, you know . . . one guy opened a transvestite bar in Milan. There were twenty-nine people doing the script collectively and after two days, three-quarters of those guys were at the beach and Jean-Luc and I were alone doing that film, which took us six months to put together. But the main thing we've been facing is the total unwillingness of people to get into any cinema of analysis, I mean, any cinema that will flatten down all fictional elements and just try to reflect on the combinations of two or three elements. There is nothing more abstract than film; abstraction, *per se*, is not something that dooms you; you can use it to go back into your life; you can use it as a tool. And that's what we were trying to do. And that's what people were not really ready to accept. Maybe they were right. I'm not as sure as I was four years ago when we had very definite ideas of love and respect for political cinema.

Q. So now you're moving into a new cinematic space?

J-P.G. Yes, I want to get into something purely fictional, science fiction. The kind of thing William Burroughs does in literature. Do you know Ishmael Reed? She's a black writer, incredibly powerful, incredibly good. She wrote a book called *Mumbo Jumbo*, in which there's a beautiful quote that science fiction films could be the only really political films ever made.

Q. There's a way of doing science fiction as a kind of satire. Are you going to do that kind of thing?

J-P.G.   Yeah, kind of. There's a lot of fantasy in the book I'm working on. But there's a problem, because years back I started writing poetry, things like that. And there's a point when writing gets its own specificity, whether it's good or bad — but it's a physical feeling. I mean, you know when you've written a page that really holds itself without any value judgment. And when it comes to writing for films, this is a trap, because when you've reached that specificity there is no point in filming it. But if you take a really bad science fiction — I mean, that's a treat and it's full of hope; you can do whatever you want. There's a lot of visual things you can build. So one of the problems I've had was not to do all the writing myself, to let others shape it. And in the meantime I've been into seeing a lot of «B» movies and a lot of science fiction movies of the 50s, you know, the McCarthy-type movies. And I've discovered that's the type of movie that really appeals to me much more than any so-called masterpiece because there are flaws in them, you can cross them, you can sleep if you want to and then come back and it's another story. That's a good thing. *Tout va bien* is like that.

I really discovered nice films like *Two Thousand Maniacs* and *Pussycat Kill Kill.* They're really something. The greatest film-maker I know in the States is Russ Meyer. He's a total schizoid. He does his editing absolutely on energy waves and at some points you can't even hear the dialogue. And it's so phoney that you just have small segments of very stock phrases which come into your head and it's absolutely hilarious. *Beyond the Valley of the Dolls* is a fantastic film and it's interesting. Gives you so many ideas.

I was reading about big catastrophe films, like *Earthquake,* so we wrote a script called *The Rise and Fall of the American Dollar.* It took five minutes on film. And it's only one shot. It's a huge accident. Started with a small thing like a dog biting a leg — you know, B52 in the street. We'll never be able to do it. It was supposed to use as many stars as possible from George C. Scott to Linda Lovelace. It's a very funny script. I played with a series of scripts like that. I wrote a story about Columbus which is real fun but we should be shooting it like a pirate movie, the kind of movie that Errol Flynn was in, like *Captain Blood* and things like that, and *Mutiny on the Bounty.* It's a pornographic film. It's a film about imperialism and about the West. And the subject of the film was the madness of Columbus. Think about that guy starting on the basis that the earth was round, which is kind of crazy — why not stay home? — when everybody was certain that the earth was flat. It was a beautiful script but impossible to do because it's a 5 million dollar script with all the Indians and the conquest and the slow dream of two thousand extras right on the spot — things like that.

But I don't think you'll get back into low budgets. All the hopes we had in '68 for an alternative distribution system really failed — fell through — and we're back into a situation where the money goes to big productions or medium low productions with name stars. And that implies the traditional type of fiction and the traditional type of narrative. When you are a film-maker you discover at one point that you *don't* do the films — which is the beginning of *Tout va bien*; I mean, the ones who really ultimately do the films are the distributors who tell you: «Well, if you want the money, you need to have such-and-such names, you need to have such-and-such type of narrative.» And from that moment on you're allowed to fool around in a certain area which is defined elsewhere. But I can handle that now. I'd like to get Al Pacino for my film, and I think the time is right for fiction once again, at least for me.

The way I relate to life and to politics is I need tales, I need tales to be told about the life I live. But at the same time each tale, when the tale is told, is like a big laugh coming out. Because the thing I'm interested in is the part where the tale breaks. What I have said about my life — and because I have said that, because I have progressed through that — suddenly reveals itself as totally irrelevant. And then I'm obliged to build a new tale and say, «Well, no, that wasn't it. Let's put the pawns of the game in another order.»

Q. So what's the biggest change in your life since 1972?

J-P.G. I'm not serious any more. Which means that I'm more serious than I was. And more playful. Want some tap dance?

A version of this interview originally appeared in *Take One,* January 1976, and is published in its present form by kind permission.

Draft Outline: The Brechtian Aspect of Radical Cinema

Chapter One: BRECHT AND THE CINEMA

The nature of Brecht's relationship with the cinema is many-faceted. In the first place, he used film within his theatrical productions. At the end of *Mother Courage,* for instance, Mother marches in front of a screen on which footage is projected from *October* and *The End of St. Petersburg.* Film is here used by Brecht to disrupt conventional stage «illusionism» in much the same manner as his use of songs to break the continuity of the action.

Secondly, Brecht worked on films in both Germany (*Threepenny Opera,* 1931 and *Whither Germany?*, 1932) and America (*Hangmen Also Die,* 1941; *Arch of Triumph,* 1947, among others). With the possible exception of *Whither Germany?,* Brecht saw the films resulting from his scripts as total betrayals of his aesthetic. But these encounters are worthy of close examination, since the problems Brecht confronted illuminate the schism between his aesthetic and that of the narrative film tradition as it mainly evolved in Europe and America.

Thirdly, Brecht's initial formulation of his theories of epic theatre was influenced by his admiration of two film artists: Charles Chaplin (his episodic narrative technique, his use of gestural acting, besides his emphasis on humour and low-life settings) and Sergei Eisenstein.

Chapter Two: THE GROWTH OF AN ANTI-ILLUSIONIST AESTHETIC

It is probably more precise to say that it wasn't so much Eisenstein himself who influenced Brecht's development, as it was the theatrical and cinematic praxis of a whole constellation of Soviet artists: Meyerhold, Mayakovsky, Tretyakov, Eisenstein, Vertov, etc. The key figure is Meyerhold; his work has only recently arisen from the tombs of Stalinist purges, and so it is only now that we are able to evaluate his significance not only as Eisenstein's mentor, but as the true precursor of Brecht's dramatic theories. In many ways, Meyerhold is the first theorist of an anti-illusionist aesthetic for the dramatic arts, and his influence not only on the development of the Soviet cinema (many of his students later worked in the cinema), but on the style of creative thought of the period (cf. *Lef* and *Novy Lef* articles) clearly filtered through to Brecht himself (he met Eisenstein in 1929) in his encounters with the Soviet art of the twenties.

Eisenstein's films (particularly *Strike* and *October*) provided splendid examples of this «anti-illusionist» aesthetic in operation. And the official reaction to *October* was one of condemnation («massive subjectivism» etc.), just as Meyerhold's theatres were closed again and again as punishment for his straying from the accepted paths of theatrical production. All through the twenties, the «anti-illusionist» artists were fighting desperately against a coagulating bureaucracy. By the thirties, total suppression was under way: Meyerhold and Tretyakov were assassinated, Mayakovsky was forced to suicide, and most other radical artists lost their freedom to work – Eisenstein, Vertov, Medvedkin. Further, much of what had been achieved was removed from public gaze (e.g. Meyerhold's name eradicated from official histories of Soviet theatre), so that by the late thirties Brecht seemed to be an isolated genius of the European avant-garde. Only now can we perceive him to be the brilliant representative of a style of thinking, a strand of aesthetic history that runs from the Soviet revolution through to May '68 and beyond.

Chapter Three: DZIGA VERTOV AND ALEKSANDR MEDVEDKIN

The work of both these directors has only recently re-emerged from years of near-total obscurity. In Medvedkin's case, his astonishing film, *Happiness* (1934), was rediscovered at the Belgian Cinémathèque in 1967, and from this the tale of the 1930–33 cine-trains also came to light. In Vertov's case, the existence of his work has been acknowledged, but no-one, until the last few years, was able to perceive the extraordinary brilliance of a film like *Man with a Movie Camera* (1929), which can only be assessed adequately through a Brechtian/anti-illusionist perspective.

For both Vertov and Medvedkin, one of the essential precepts of their creative activity is a direct relationship between audience and film-maker, though this precept manifests itself in different ways. Vertov, for instance, underlines the film-maker's task as being simply that of a proletarian worker among others, in *Man with a Movie Camera,* while Medvedkin's work on the cine-train was devoted to making film an actual tool in the changing of the social fabric – travelling from town to town, filming «advanced» work and «retarded» work, then screening the films to the very subjects of the films.

Medvedkin's *Happiness* is a brilliant didactic comedy, in the spirit of Chaplin, and represents perhaps the only great radical comedy in film history – the film that Brecht might have wished Chaplin to make.

Chapter Four: BRECHT AND JEAN-LUC GODARD

Brecht's influence on a seminal group of European film-makers since 1960 has been incalculable, and the central figure is without doubt that of Godard, whose total *oeuvre* constitutes a superbly «Brechtian» evolution: i.e. a refusal of doctrine, the insistence on questions rather than answers. And this questioning concerns both the nature of the aesthetic artefact (what is film? what is theatre?) and the nature of its relationship to society and social issues. The notion of artistic creation as a socially engaged activity, and of the experience of art as an intellectually stimulating (rather than emotionally fulfilling) activity is central to Godard's endeavour; indeed his progression from an a-political standpoint to one of political engagement parallels Brecht's own evolution.

Godard's films are replete with direct references to Brecht, and quotations from Brecht (*Le Mépris, Deux ou trois choses que je sais d'elle, La Chinoise, Tout va bien,* etc.) and, more crucially, employ Brechtian devices with great trenchancy, whether it be the use of «*tableau*» settings in *Tout va bien,* the insertion of «titles» throughout the narrative of *La Chinoise* (*Pierrot le fou, Weekend,* etc.); frequently Godard adapts Brechtian notions to a specifically cinematic realisation – his development of the lateral tracking shot to establish a critical distance between viewer and the events on the screen, for instance, and his increasing rejection of «depth of field» (itself a basic «illusionist» technique) provide instances of this.

Chapter Five: SUBVERSIVE CINEMA: DUSAN MAKAVEJEV

Godard's films through the 1960's were a response to, and reflected, the increasing tensions within French society and thought, and forced a re-evaluation of the social context of film; his pioneering work was a source of inspiration to a number of other film-makers who, in their own very different ways continued to create films that took as their specific task the interrogation of the relationship between art and the social fabric. One of the most exciting personalities is that of Yugoslavian Dusan Makavejev, whose films have increasingly tended toward a provocative subversion of our normative conceptions of reality, both textually and behaviourally. That is to say, *WR: Mysteries of the Organism* (1970), for instance, is constructed from film-footage of very different origins — archive, documentary, ciné-vérité, conventional narrative — all of which is brilliantly blended into a whole that defies any passive acceptance of the «truthfulness» of cinematic images — the «illusion of reality» cracks before our very eyes; and both *WR* and the recent *Sweet Movie* take sexual mores as their central theme, and deliberately work to shock the audience out of their complacency. Reassessment of one's own situation, attitudes, and beliefs is demanded by Makavejev's sharply satiric eye. His emphasis on the liberating power of humour also reiterates his connections with Brecht (and, indeed, Medvedkin).

Chapter Six: ASCETIC CINEMA: JEAN-MARIE STRAUB

Jean-Marie Straub is in many respects the cinematic antithesis of Makavejev, but his work is nevertheless equally founded on Brechtian attitudes. A much more ascetic director, whose films are undeniably «difficult», Straub's significance lies at one pole of the Brechtian aesthetic: he is by no means «populist» (something Brecht always strove for), but the ethical vigour of his aesthetic approach clearly owes much to Brecht's examples (one of his early films, *Not Reconciled* (1964–5), is prefaced by a quotation from Brecht). Most obviously, it is Straub's insistence on the audience's distance from the images on the screen that is important, his demand that we consciously examine what we are presented with, that places him within the «Brechtian school» that I am outlining.

Thematically, a substantial portion of his work is concerned with the relationship between the artist and society, the artist and politics, the artist and history, as we can see in both *The Chronicle of Anna Magdalena Bach* (1968) and *Othon* (1971). And, like Godard and Makavejev — and Vertov — his films are concerned with the nature of cinematic expression itself: filmic articulation must not hide its presence, in the manner of the illusionist cinema, but must consciously work to deconstruct the «norms» of the Hollywood narrative tradition (cf. *The Bridegroom, The Comedienne, and the Pimp,* 1968). In this, of course, Straub is in harmony with Brecht's desire to deconstruct «lyric» theatre, in order to set up its opposite, the «epic» theatre.

Finally, Straub's *History Lessons* (1972) is based on Brecht's novelistic fragment, *The Business Deals of Mr Julius Caesar,* and thus marks an absolutely explicit engagement with the tasks confronting a Brechtian film-maker.

Martin Walsh: Biography and Articles published

MARTIN WALSH: BIOGRAPHY AND PUBLISHED ARTICLES
Born July 1947, Kent, England. Eleven years of school life were spent at St Dunstans College, London, where time was divided with difficulty between classroom, sportsfield and a set of rock and roll drums. English Literature was a more serious study: Martin graduated with a BA(Hons) from the University of Exeter (1969) followed by an MA from the University of Kent, England (1970). His thesis at Kent was on the work of the French writer *Alfred Jarry*.

This was followed by two years at the Film Studies Department of the Slade School of Fine Art (London). During this time he wrote a thesis on the films of *Ingmar Bergman*, articles for the film journal, *Monogram*, and was a contributor to the *Oxford Companion to Film*.

In 1972 he became a Lecturer in Film Studies at the University of Western Ontario, Canada, and an Assistant Professor in 1974. He wrote numerous articles for film journals in Canada, the USA and England, and revised and expanded the «cinema» entries for the sixth edition of the *Everyman Encyclopaedia*. He was responsible for the planning and implementation of a Film Research Centre, which was established at the university in 1976, and was President of the Film Studies Association of Ontario from 1974–7. In 1976 he received a Canada Council Grant for research on *Brecht and Film*.

In Canada he became a fanatical cyclist and raced with the London Centennial Wheelers. Returning from a training session in the summer of 1977, he was tragically struck by a car on the open highway and killed. He was due to return to England from Canada to take up a teaching post at the University of Kent.

Articles published
«Ermanno Olmi: the ethic of individual responsibility», *Monogram* No. 2, 1971.
«John Boorman's *Leo the Last*», *Monogram*, No. 3, 1972.
«Bo Widerberg», *Gaslight*, February 1972.
«Film at the University of Western Ontario», *Screen Education Notes*, Autumn 1973.
«During the Summer: Ermanno Olmi», *Gaslight*, Summer 1973.
«*Little Big Man:* Arthur Penn», *Gaslight*, Summer 1973.
«Dusan Makavejev's *WR: Mysteries of the Organism*», *Monogram*, No. 5, Summer 1974.
«The Complex Seer: Brecht and the Film», *Sight and Sound*, Autumn 1974.
«Political Formations in the Cinema of Jean-Marie Straub», *Jump Cut*, No. 4, 1974.
«Losey, Brecht and *Galileo*», *Jump Cut*, No. 7, 1975.
«Antonioni's Narrative Design», *Jump Cut*, No. 8, 1975.
«Godard and Me (Jean-Pierre Gorin Talks)», *Take One*, January 1976.
«Brecht and the Cinema», transcript of the 1975 Edinburgh Film Festival Brecht Event, *Screen*, Vol. 16, No. 4, Winter 1975–6.

«Noël Burch's Film Theory», *Jump Cut,* Nos. 10/11, 1976.
«*Moses and Aaron* — Straub and Huillet's Schoenberg», *Jump Cut,* Nos. 12/13, 1977.
«Structural Ambiguities in the Films of Erich Rohmer», *Film Criticism,* No. 2, September 1976.
«*Introduction to Arnold Schoenberg's ‹Accompaniment for a Cinematographic Scene›* Straub/Huillet: Brecht: Schoenberg», *Camera Obscura,* No. 2, Fall 1977 (published posthumously).
«The Political Joke in *Happiness*», *Screen,* Vol. 19, No. 1, Spring 1978 (published posthumously).
«On Re-evaluating Rossellini», *Jump Cut,* No. 15, 1977.
«*History Lessons:* Brecht and Straub/Huillet: The Frontiers of Language», *Afterimage* No. 7, Spring 1977.

Drawing of Martin Walsh by Greg Curnoe

References

Adorno, T. W., *Prisms,* Spearman, St Helier, Jersey 1967.
Bann, S., *Ian Hamilton Finlay: an illustrated essay,* Scottish National Gallery, Edinburgh 1972.
Barthes, R., *Critical Essays,* Northwestern University Press, Evanston, Illinois 1972.
Barthes, R., «Brecht, Diderot, Eisenstein», *Screen,* Vol. 15, No. 2, Summer 1974.
Barthes, R., *The Pleasure of the Text,* translated by Richard Miller, Hill and Wang, New York 1975.
Bazin, A., *What is Cinema?,* Vol. 2, translated by Hugh Gray, University of California Press, Berkeley 1971.
Benjamin, W., *Illuminations,* edited by Hannah Arendt, NLB, London 1969.
Benjamin, W., *Understanding Brecht,* NLB, London 1970.
Bogdanov, A., «Puti proletarskogo tvorchestra», *O proletarskoi kulture,* Leningrad, Moscow 1924.
Braun, E. (*ed.* and *transl.*), *Meyerhold on Theatre,* Hill and Wang, New York 1969.
Brecht, B., *Brecht on Theatre,* edited by John Willett, Hill and Wang, New York 1964(a).
Brecht, B., *The Threepenny Opera,* translated by D. Vesey, Grove Press, New York 1964(b); also published by Eyre Methuen, London 1973.
Brecht, B., *Sur le cinéma,* Editions l'Arche, Paris 1970, quoted and translated by Julia Lesage in *Cineaste,* Vol. V, No. 2, Spring 1972.
Brecht, B., 1973, see Leiser, 1973.
Brecht, B., *Collected Poems,* Parts 1–3, edited by John Willett, Eyre Methuen, London 1976.
Brewster, B., «Brecht and the Film Industry», *Screen,* Vol. 16, No. 4, Winter 1975–6.
Burch, N., *Theory of Film Practice,* Secker and Warburg, London 1973.
Burch, N., «An Interview with Noël Burch», *Women and Film,* Vol. 1, Nos. 5–6, 1974.
Eisenstein, S. M., «Letter from S. M. Eisenstein», *Image et Son,* No. 255, Dec 1971.
Eisler, H., 1975, see Witt, 1975.
Eisner, L. H., *The Haunted Screen,* Thames and Hudson, London 1969.
Eley, R., «A History of the Scratch Orchestra», in *Stockhausen Serves Imperialism,* edited by Cornelius Cardew, Latimer New Dimensions, London 1974.
Freud, S., *Jokes and their Relation to the Unconscious,* Standard Edition of the Complete Psychological Works, Vol. III (1905), Hogarth Press, London 1951; Penguin, Harmondsworth, Middlesex 1976.
Heath, S., «Preface to Reading *S/Z*», in *Signs of the Times,* edited by Stephen Heath, Colin MacCabe, Christopher Prendergast, Granta, Cambridge 1972.
Heath, S., «From Brecht to Film: Theses, Problems», *Screen,* Vol. 16, No. 4, Winter 1975–6.
Leiser, E., *Ecran,* No. 13, March 1973.

Leyda, J., *Kino,* Allen and Unwin, London 1960.
Losey, J., *Losey on Losey,* interviewed by Tom Milne, Secker and Warburg, London 1967.
Marker, C., «Le ciné-ours», *Image et Son,* No. 255, December 1971.
Meyerhold, 1969, see Braun, 1969.
Novy Lef, Nos. 11/12, 1927, editorial, translated by Diana Matias, in *Screen,* Vol. 12, No. 4, Winter 1971.
Reich, W., *Schoenberg: a critical biography,* Longman, London 1971.
Reich, 1975, see Witt, 1975.
Roberts, K. H. and Sharples, W., *A Primer for Film-making,* Pegasus, New York 1971.
Rosen, C., *Arnold Schoenberg,* Viking Press, New York 1975.
Roud, R., *Straub,* Cinema One Series, Secker and Warburg, London 1971.
Schoenberg, A., in *Schoenberg* (1937), edited by Merle Armitage, Greenwood, Westport, Connecticut 1975.
Schoenberg, A., *Schoenberg's Letters,* edited by Erwin Stein, Faber and Faber, London 1964; paperback 1974.
Schrader, P., «Ozu Spectrum», *Cinema* (USA), Vol. 6, No. 1, 1970.
Schrader, P., «The Rise of Louis XIV», *Cinema* (USA), Vol. 6, No. 3, 1970.
Schrader, P., *Transcendental Style on Film: Ozu, Bresson, Dreyer,* University of California Press, Berkeley 1972.
Schumacher, E., «The Dialectics of *Galileo*», in *Brecht,* edited by E. Munk, Bantam, New York 1972.
Straub, J–M., interviewed by Andi Engel, *Cinemantics,* No. 1, 1970.
Straub, J–M., 1976, see Straub and Huillet 1976.
Straub, J–M. and Huillet, D., *Journal of the Royal College of Art,* January 1976.
Vaughan James, C., *Soviet Socialist Realism,* Macmillan, London 1973.
Vertov, Dziga, *Lef,* Vol. 3, translated by Richard Sherwood in *Screen,* Vol. 12, No. 4, Winter 1971.
Witt, H. (*ed.*), *Brecht As They Knew Him,* Lawrence and Wishart, London 1975.
Wollen, P., *Signs and Meaning in the Cinema,* Cinema One Series, Secker and Warburg, London 1972.

Further Reading

Brecht, B., *18 Critical Pieces from the TDR,* edited by Erika Munk, Bantam, New York 1972.
Brecht, B., *Sur le cinéma,* Editions l'Arche, Paris 1970.
Brecht, B., *Sur le réalisme,* Editions l'Arche, Paris 1970.
Brecht, B., *Kuhle Wampe,* edited by Wolfgang Gersch and Werner Hecht, Suhrkamp Verlag, Frankfurt am Main 1969.

Brecht, B., *Brecht on Theatre,* edited by John Willett, Hill and Wang, New York 1964.
Brecht, B., «Against Georg Lukács», in Bloch, E. *et al., Aesthetics and Politics,* NLB, London 1977.
Volker, Klaus, *Brecht Chronicle,* Seabury, New York 1975.
Screen, Vol. 15, No. 2, Summer 1974 and Vol. 16, No. 4, Winter 1975–6: special issues on Brecht.
Witt, H. (*ed.*), *Brecht As They Knew Him,* Lawrence and Wishart, London 1975.
Benjamin, W., *Understanding Brecht,* NLB, London 1973.
Benjamin, W., *Illuminations,* edited by Hannah Arendt, NLB, London 1969; Fontana/Collins, London 1970.
Barthes, R., *L'Empire des signes,* Albert Skirra, Paris 1970.
Willett, J., *The New Sobriety: Art and Politics in the Weimar Period (1917–33),* Thames and Hudson, London 1978.
Braun, E. (*ed.* and *transl.*), *Meyerhold on Theatre,* Hill and Wang, New York 1969.
Paris – Berlin (1900–33), Centre national d'art et de culture Georges Pompidou, Paris 1978, exhibition catalogue.
Paris–Moscow (1900–33), Centre national d'art et de culture Georges Pompidou, Paris 1979, exhibition catalogue.
Art in Revolution: Soviet Art and Design Since 1917, Arts Council of Great Britain, London 1971, Hayward Gallery exhibition catalogue.
Roud, R., *Straub,* Cinema One Series, Secker and Warburg, London 1971.
Engel, A. (*ed.*), «Straub*Huillet», in *Enthusiasm,* No. 1, 1975.
MacCabe, C., *Godard: Images, Sounds, Politics,* British Film Institute/Macmillan Press, London 1980.
Harvey, S., *May '68 and Film Culture,* British Film Institute, London 1978.
Bann, S., *Ian Hamilton Finlay: an illustrated essay,* Scottish National Gallery, Edinburgh 1972.
Eisler, H., *A Rebel in Music: Selected Writings,* edited by Manfred Grabs, Seven Seas Books, Berlin 1978.
Rosen, C., *Schoenberg,* Fontana Modern Masters, London 1976.
Maegaard, J., *Studien zur Entwicklung des dodekaphonen Satzes bei Arnold Schoenberg,* Wilhelm Hansen, Copenhagen 1972.
Schoenberg/Gerhard Series Programme (The London Sinfonietta, Oct–Nov 1973), including essays by Arnold Whittal, Alexander Goehr, Roberto Gerhard, Hans Keller, Michael Tippett, Sinfonietta Productions, London 1973.
Hodeir, A., *Since Debussy: a view of contemporary music,* translated by Noël Burch, Grove Press, New York 1961.
Afterimage, Nos. 1–7, an occasional publication from London.